All about the Shetland Sheepdog

Frontispiece:
The author with some
of her Riverhills in
1979.

All about
the Shetland Sheepdog

Felicity M. Rogers

PELHAM BOOKS

First published in Great Britain by
Pelham Books Ltd
44 Bedford Square
London WC1B 3DU
1974

Second Revised Edition August 1980

Rogers, Felicity Margaret
    All about the Shetland sheepdog. — 2nd
    revised ed.
    1. Shetland sheep-dogs
    I. Title
    636.7'3   SF429–S62

ISBN 0 7207 1222 X

Typeset by Cambrian Typesetters, Farnborough, Hants

Dedicated to Clara Bowring for all she has done for the breed and the E.S.S.C. And to Patience whose flair for picking puppies has played such a large part in the making of the Riverhills

Acknowledgements

My thanks to D. M. Heeley, MRCVS for his help in the First Aid chapter, and to Mrs Marriage, Mrs Upton, Mr A. Adamson and Mr W.G. Russell for their help with some of the illustrations.

Contents

Illustrations

LINE DRAWINGS

PICTURE CREDITS

Author's Note

All that is written here is the result of forty-nine years' experience breeding Shelties. Nothing is recommended that we do not do or have not done; and it has worked with our dogs. In fact, we practise what we preach.

I should like to say to prospective breeders: always remember that dogs are not machines, and nature has a way of dealing you a backhander if you flout it. Every year we have been breeding something has happened that never happened before. So do not, after a year or two, however successful you have been, think you know it all. If you do, you will suddenly turn a corner and find yourself in a slough of despondency. Equally, if everything goes wrong, soldier on and if you stick to it your luck is bound to change. Everybody, even the most successful breeders, has their lean periods and it is these periods that sort the men from the boys.

F. M. ROGERS

1   Origin and History

The origins of the Shetland Sheepdog are rather obscure and a good deal has to be taken on trust; one has only to look at an atlas to see that the Shetland Islands are the most northern part of the British Isles, about halfway between Scotland and Norway. In fact, at one time they belonged to Norway and were part of the dowry of a princess who married a Scottish king. So it is quite reasonable to suppose that Norse dogs played a part in the make-up of the original Sheltie: the pale wheaten colour that turns up in the breed could well come from the Norwegian Buhund as this colour is unknown in Collies.

It has recently come to my knowledge that there may also be some Dutch origin behind the Sheltie. The Dutch herring fishers, or Hollanders as they were known, used to visit the islands as early as the fifteenth century and they helped in the founding of Lerwick. From 1866 onwards they visited Bressay Sound every weekend during the herring season right up till the 1914 war. During this long period I feel Dutch dogs must have visited with their masters.

Shelties must owe their make and shape to the working Collie from the Scottish mainland and also the ability to work sheep which is still strong in some of the modern dogs. A notable example was Ch. Dilhorne Norseman of Melvaig who belonged to a farmer and worked a flock of 300 sheep. He was the Best of Breed winner at Cruft's in 1955 and Best in Show at the E.S.S.C. (English Shetland Sheepdog Club) championship show the same year, a remarkable double only achieved twice since — once by his grandson Ch. Riverhill Rogue in 1960, and by Ch. Riverhill Richman in 1969.

The Yakki dog from Iceland is said to be responsible for the smutty muzzles that turn up now and then. Last but not least, a black and tan King Charles Spaniel, who got left behind by a visiting yacht, appears to have played quite an important part in the Sheltie's make-up. There are two points to show that this isn't just a figment of the imagination. The first is that by far the largest number of dogs registered in the first *Stud Book* of the Shetland Club were black and tans, a colour that has now died out. The second is also a colour factor: two tricolour Shelties can produce a clear gold sable, a thing impossible in Collies, whereas two black and tan King Charles Spaniels can produce rubies.

Shelties in their time have had many names: Toonie dogs, because

Detail from 'Lerwick from the Stony Hill' by John Frome R.S.A., 1840. Note the Sheltie in the foreground.

Early Shelties in Shetland. Note the likeness to the dog in the previous picture.

the crofts are known as toons; Shetland Collies; Peerie dogs (small); Shetland Sheepdogs. Now their pet name of Sheltie is the most common. On the islands, they are still called Shetland Collies but when the breed was first recognised by the Kennel Club the Collie clubs objected so strongly to them being called Collies that the Kennel Club gave way and changed the name to Sheepdogs.

One amusing story was about a Collie breeder who said he could pick a dog out of the streets and make it a Shetland Sheepdog champion. This he proceeded to do and the result was Ch. Freshfield Fad, the foundation bitch of Family 16 (See p. 104).

The Royal Navy played an important part in introducing the Shetland Sheepdog to the mainland. When the Grand Fleet was on manoeuvres, the sailors went ashore on the islands and bought puppies to send home to their families. The Shetland pony dealers also brought over the dogs to the mainland. One of the most important dealers was Mr Graham Clark of the Ashbank Shelties, a pioneer of the breed; his famous Ch. Ashbank Actress had her pictures on the cover of the first two E.S.S.C. handbooks. I was lucky enough to see this lovely sable bitch. Admittedly she was middle-aged but even so she was outstanding. Her son, Arthur of Camelaird, sired several champions.

The demand for fluffy puppies grew so that everybody started breeding from anything that would give them saleable puppies. People on the islands who had the good of the breed at heart got together and formed the Shetland Collie Club at Lerwick in 1908 and started a *Stud Book*. The Scottish Club was started in 1909 but it was not until 1914 that the English Shetland Sheepdog Club was formed. This club has gone from strength to strength: in 1935 there were 56 members, in 1974 over 800, and in 1979 over 1,100.

My first introduction to the Sheltie was in 1914 when, as a child, I visited an uncle and aunt in Northumberland who had a Sheltie called Rene, a small tricolour with low ears and a round head. She seemed to spend most of the time rolling on her back. She must have made an impression as I can still remember what she looked like. But it was not a case of love at first sight as my heart was set on a Border Collie and I thought a Sheltie a poor substitute. It was not till seventeen years later that I bought my first Sheltie, and that was to mate to a Border; incidentally an event that never took place but got me into the show ring instead.

The Kennel Club gave the breed a separate classification in 1914, not a very auspicious moment! In 1915, the first Challenge Certificate was awarded at Birmingham show and was won by Mrs Huband's Frea. Later the Kennel Club clamped down on shows and breeding. Puppies born in the latter part of the war could not be registered. For a breed just starting, this was a sad setback and by the time the war was over and breeding could start again the breed was in a pretty poor state. Some working stock remained in the islands and in Aberdeenshire, but Miss Thynne (Kilvarock), Miss Humphries (Mountfort) and Miss Grey (Greyhills) were about the only English breeders to have any stock left.

Miss Humphries saw that something desperate must be done and she obtained a small Collie called Teena who was mated to Wallace, the son of Butcher Boy who is the foundation of the male Line BB. This mating produced War Baby of Mountfort from whom all present-day BB's are descended. Teena was then sold to Mr J. G. Saunders (Helensdale). If you look at Family 10 (See p. 101) you will see that Ch. Gawaine of Camelaird was one of her descendants. He played a large part in our interest in the breed and was the sire of our first litter. Miss Humphries made no mystery about her Collie cross, unlike some later breeders who kept everything very hush hush so one has to guess at what took place.

In the early 1920s Mr Caird of Aberdeen bred the famous Chestnut litter which produced Chestnut Rainbow from whom all the CHE Line descends. Mr Pierce also started his Eltham Park kennel about this time. He swept the board, producing eighteen C.C. (Challenge Certificate) winners between 1923–35. Ten of them were champions, and it must be remembered at that time there were nothing like the number of championship shows with C.C.s for the breed. In fact, there were nine in 1935 compared with thirty-four in 1979.

The most important Eltham Park champion was Eureka, who played a very large part in the BB Line. Mr Pierce shipped most of his winners out to the U.S.A. to Miss Fry. Unfortunately for the breed in the States, they were hardly bred from. What a waste from both countries' point of view as they were real quality dogs.

In the middle twenties a great deal of controversy went on among the breeders who wanted long Collie heads and those who wanted the old island type. But in 1927 two dogs were produced who combined the two groups: Ch. Helensdale Laddie, who later went to America to Mr Gallagher of Page's Hill and Ch. Gawaine of Camelaird. This was followed in 1928 and 1929 by some very important dogs: Miss Tod's Ch. Max of Clerwood; Mr and Mrs Cambell's Ch. Tilford Tontine (the top brood bitch until Ch. Riverhill Rare Gold took over in the 1950s), Ch. Euan of Clerwood and the great Ch. Uam Var of Houghton Hill, a dog whose influence is still with us.

In 1929 Miss Clara Bowring took over the English Shetland Sheepdog Club and became secretary. Things took a turn for the better and the breed really began to get somewhere. From then until 1939 there were some really first class dogs produced, notably Ch.s Uam Var of Houghton Hill, Mime of Houghton Hill C.C. winner, Orchis of Houghton Hill and Nutkin of Houghton Hill; Ch.s Moneyspinner and Spendthrift of Exford, Ch. Riverhill Rufus, Ch. Catmore Chum, Ch. Wrennie of Wyndora,

Arthur of Camelaird, Ch. Fetlar Magnus, Ch. Rob Roy O'Page's Hill who started life as a Helensdale and had his name changed. Thank heavens that is not allowed now; it made pedigree-keeping very difficult. There was one bitch who had litters under three different names. Luckily she wasn't a Sheltie.

The outstanding bitches of this period were Ch.s Blue Blossom and Zephyr of Houghton Hill; Ch. Tilford Tontine who I have mentioned before as being the largest winner-producer; Ch. Eltham Park Elda, one that did not go overseas; Ch. Peabody Peggoty, Ch. Peaceful, Ellington Dainty Lady, Ch. Wevonne of Wyndora; Ch.s Michelmore Sona and Daffin; Riverhill Romantic and her daughter Riverhill Rosalind who with Enchantress of Inchmery didn't quite make their titles before the war started.

They all bred on. Ch. Jenny Wren of Crawleyridge, Enchantress's little sister, did make it but was shipped to the U.S.A. — with her kennel mates Laird of Exford, Toonie Bridget of Crawleyridge and Ch. Catmore Chum — by their owner Col. the Hon. B. Russell who thought they would be safer there. As it turned out, no bombs fell near Crawleyridge so they would have been quite safe.

At the end of the last war, Shetland Sheepdogs were in a much stronger position than they were after the first great war. For one thing, the Kennel Club had not clamped down on breeding and although there were no championship shows there were lots of open, limited and sanction ones that people could go to at weekends.

After the war, the first championship shows were breed ones. They did not need such large halls and the Kennel Club rightly thought that the individual breeds should be got going first.

Actually, the first E.S.S.C. show was held in 1945. It was an open show, judged by Miss Bowring. Nuthatch of Larchwood was best in show. He later became the first post-war champion dog. The next year we had a championship show which my sister, Patience Rogers, judged. The C.C.s were won by Magnum of Exford, and Ellington Enjoyment who was Best in Show and later became the first post-war bitch champion.

1947 saw Ch. Nuthatch of Larchwood, who was a blue merle, made up (became a champion); and Ch. Riverhill Redcoat too. Both dogs have left their mark in future generations. In bitches, besides Ch. Ellington Enjoyment, Ch. Bonfire of Exford was made up. She was a really lovely little tricolour who has bred on.

In 1948, the E.S.S.C. decided to bring out a *Handbook*. They had produced one in 1933 and again in 1935 but now a momentous decision was taken: to trace back all the C.C. winners in tail male and tail female line. The female families were numbered and the male lines were given letters — CHE and BB, etc. Miss M. Osborne took on this huge undertaking and a right good job she made of it. I think the charts of Lines

Five Shelties in 1914, owned by Mrs Huband. *From left:* Jason, Lerwick, Freyja, unknown, Lerwick Jarl, and unknown.

and Families are more or less unique to the E.S.S.C. I do not believe that any other breed except Collies has had this done. And the Collies are Miss Osborne's work too.

Since the first *Handbook* was brought out in 1948, there have been many more. All subsequent charts have been my business. The C.C. winners have grown from 195 to 582. To the serious breeder they are invaluable, the only trouble being that they are now so vast they will soon want a volume to themselves.

Once the general championship shows started, the club show reverted to being an open show. It was not until 1952 that it was elevated to championship status again. This time, Miss Bowring judged. The dog C.C. went to Ch. Riverhill Rescuer and the bitch to a blue merle, Vennards Benedictine. She was the most wonderful colour. Unfortunately for her proud owners, soon after this great win where she was Best in Show, she developed distemper and died.

Incidentally, this win caused a change to be made in the E.S.S.C. rules regarding cup and special winners. Benedictine was owned in partnership by Mr and Mrs Joy and they took all the cups and specials that

were either for the best owned by a gentleman or best owned by a lady. It was decided that mixed sex partnerships could not win these; in future partnerships had to be both the same sex to win.

The breed kept on going from strength to strength. In 1948 Miss Bowring retired from being secretary and took on the club chairmanship, a role she filled in the most splendid fashion. Miss Day Currie became E.S.S.C. secretary and her Scotch thriftiness built up the club funds so that it was possible to bring out a *Handbook* about every five years.

The breed continued to grow in popularity; I think it was helped on by the Lassie films. So many children wanted a Lassie and parents boggled at a full size Collie and said they would have to be content with a miniature Lassie. Walking a Sheltie in the streets you heard young voices saying, 'Oh look, a little Lassie' instead of what we used to hear: 'Oh what's that? Is it a fox?'

In some ways it was nice to have the breed rise up in the Kennel Club tables to seventh place, but with the added interest comes the drawback

Former Houghton Hill champions owned by Mrs E. Baker: Ch. Blue Blossom (1933), Ch. Mazurka (1935), Ch. Uam Var (1930) and Ch. Peablossom (1933).

of the puppy factories stepping in and people keeping twenty and thirty bitches, breeding from them at every heat, using some scruffy dog of no merit, and flooding the market with really bad specimens. Some that have been brought to us to mate hardly resemble a Sheltie at all. Good money has been paid for them too, and all came from dealers. It is a difficult situation to deal with and the only real thing to do is to try and educate the general public to only buy from reputable breeders.

2 The Standards

The First Standard

(NB: metric equivalents are only approximates.)

The Shetland Sheepdog Club 1908.

The type and points of the Shetland Sheepdog shall be similar to those of the Rough Collie in miniature. The height shall not exceed 15 inches (38 cm). A Register shall be kept of members' dogs from 12 to 15 inches (30—38 cm).

The Scottish Shetland Sheepdog Club 1909.

The general appearance of the Shetland Sheepdog is that of an ordinary Collie in miniature. In height about 12 inches (30—31 cm) and weight from 10—14 pounds (4.5—6.5 kg.). These are two varieties — the rough-coated and the smooth-coated. The smooth-coated dog only differs from the rough in its coat, which should be short, dense and quite smooth.

1914. The general appearance of the Shetland Sheepdog is that of the modern show Collie in miniature. (Collie character and type must be adhered to). Ideal height 12 inches (30—31 cm) at maturity which is fixed at ten months old. Smooth-coated specimens are barred.

1930. As below for English Club in 1930.

The English Shetland Sheepdog Club 1914.

The general appearance of the Shetland Sheepdog is approximately of a show Collie in miniature. Ideal height 12 inches (30—31 cm).

1923. Type confirmed but height expressed as 'from 12—15 inches (30—39 cm), the ideal height being 13½ inches (34 cm)'.

1930. General appearance altered to 'Should resemble a Collie (Rough) in miniature.

In June 1965 the E.S.S.C. Scottish Shetland Sheepdog Club and Northern Counties S.S. Club agreed on a joint Standard and it was passed by the Kennel Club.

The Standard 1965

(Reproduced by courtesy of The Kennel Club.)

Characteristics

To enable the Shetland Sheepdog to fulfil its natural bent for sheepdog work, its physical structure should be on the lines of strength and activity, free from cloddiness and without any trace of coarseness. Although the desired type is similar to that of the Rough Collie, there are marked differences that must to noted. The expression, being one of the most marked characteristics of the breed, is obtained by the perfect balance and combination of skull and foreface, size, shape, colour and placement of eyes, correct position and carriage of ears, all harmoniously blended to produce that almost indefinable look of sweet, alert, gentle intelligence.

Ch. Riverhill Real Gold, a perfectly proportioned Sheltie showing the points.

The Shetland Sheepdog should show affection and response to his

owner; he may show reserve to strangers but not to the point of nervousness.

General Appearance

The Shetland Sheepdog should instantly appeal as a dog of great beauty, intelligence and alertness. Action lithe and graceful with speed and jumping power great for its size. The outline should be symmetrical so that no part appears out of proportion to the whole. An abundance of coat, mane and frill, with shapeliness of head and sweetness of expression all combine to present the ideal Shetland Sheepdog that will inspire and secure admiration.

Head and skull. The skull should be refined and its shape when viewed from the top or side is a long blunt wedge, tapering from ear to nose. The width of the skull necessarily depends upon the combined length of skull and muzzle, and the whole must be considered in connection with the size of the dog. The skull should be flat, moderately wide between the ears, showing no prominence of the occipital bone. Cheeks should be flat and merge smoothly into a well-rounded muzzle. Skull and muzzle to be of equal length; central point to be the inner corner of the eye. In profile the topline of the skull should be parallel to the topline of the muzzle, but on a higher plane due to a slight but definite stop. Lips should be tight, teeth should be sound and level, with an evenly spaced scissor bite.

Eyes. A very important feature giving expression to the dog. They should be of medium size, obliquely set and of almond shape. Colour dark brown, except in the case of blue merles when blue is permissible.

Ears. These should be small and moderately wide at the base, placed fairly close together on top of the skull. When in repose they should be thrown back, but when on the alert brought forward and carried semi-erect with the tips dropping forward.

Neck. The neck should be muscular, well-arched and of sufficient length to carry the head proudly.

Body and quarters. From the withers the shoulder blade should slope at a 45-degree angle, forward and downward to the shoulder joint. At the withers they are separated only by the vertebrae but they must slope outwards to accommodate the desired spring of ribs. The upper arm should join the shoulder blade at as nearly a right angle as possible. The elbow joint to be equidistant from the ground and the withers. The forelegs should be straight when viewed from the front, muscular and clean, with strong bone. Pasterns should be strong and flexible. The body is slightly longer from the withers to the root of the tail than the height at the withers, but most of the length is due to the proper angulation of shoulders and hind-quarters. The chest should be deep, reaching to the

Correct scissor bite 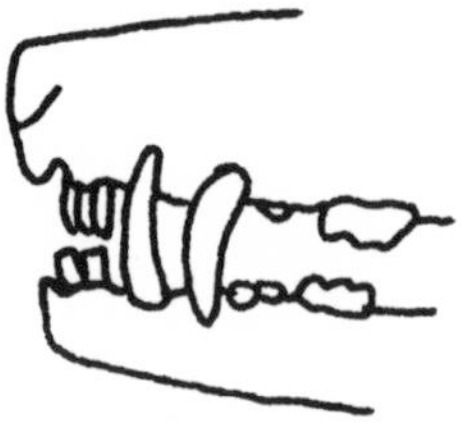   *Undershot*    *Overshot*

Upper jaw   *Lower jaw*

2 Canines
12 Molars
Total 20

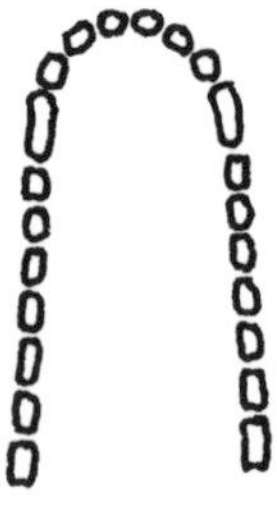

6 Incisors
2 Canines
14 Molars
Total 22

Scissor bite

Full complement 42

Correct shoulder angulation   *Wrong shoulder angulation*

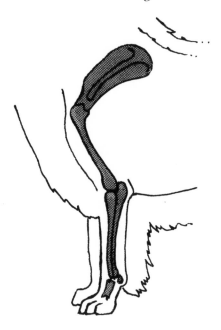 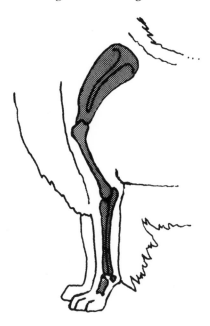

An example of good stance, correct conformation, good spring of pastern, well-bent stifle and well-let-down hocks.

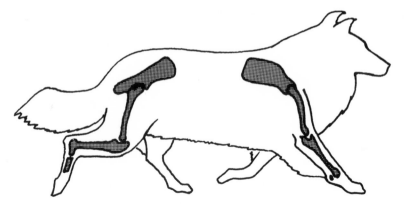

Fig. 1 Showing free movement with correct angulation

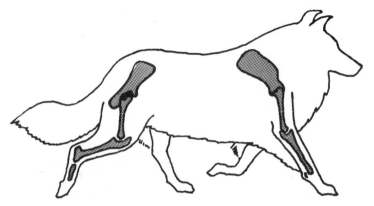

Fig. 2 Showing stilted movement with wrong angulation

point of the elbow. The ribs well-sprung but tapering at their lower half to allow free play of the forelegs and shoulders. The back should be level, with a graceful sweep over the loins and the croup should slope gradually to the rear. The thigh should be broad and muscular; the thigh bones should be set into the pelvis at right angles corresponding to the angle of the shoulder blade. The stifle joint, where the femur bone joins the tibia bone, must have a distinct angle. Hock joint should be clean cut, angular and well-let-down with strong bone. The hock must be straight when viewed from behind.

Tail. Set on low, tapering bone, must reach at least to the hock joint, with abundant hair and slight upward sweep; raised when the dog is moving, but never over the level of the back.

Feet. Oval in shape, soles well padded, toes arched and close together.

Gait. The action of the Shetland Sheepdog should denote speed and smoothness. There should be no pacing, plaiting, rolling or stiff stilted up and down movement.

Coat. Must be double, the outer coat of long hair of harsh texture and straight, the undercoat soft (resembling fur), short and close. The mane and frill should be very abundant and forelegs well feathered. Hind legs above the hocks profusely covered with hair but below the hocks fairly smooth. The mask or face smooth. What are commonly known as smooth-coated specimens are barred.

Colour

Tricolours should be an intense black on the body with no signs of ticking; rich tan markings on a tricolour to be preferred. Sables may be clear or shaded, any colour from gold to deep mahogany, but in its shade the colour should be rich in tones. Wolf sable and grey colours are undesirable. Blue merle, clear, silvery blue is desired, splashed and marbled with black. Rich tan markings to be preferred, but their absence not to be counted as a fault. Heavy black markings, slate coloured or rusty tinge in either top or undercoat is highly undesirable. General effect should be blue. White markings may be shown in the blaze, collar, chest frill, legs, stifles and tip of tail. All or some tan markings may be shown

An example of bad conformation, straight shoulder and upper arm, no spring of pastern, very straight stifle and hocks.

An example of good width of chest, good front and slope of pastern, but toeing in behind.

An example of bad front, very narrow with straight upper arm and bad cow hocks.

on eyebrows, cheeks, legs, stifles and under tail. All or some of the white markings are to be preferred whatever the colour of the dog, but the absence of these markings shall not be considered a fault. Black and white and black and tan are also recognised colours. Over-marking of patches of white on the body are highly undesirable. The nose should be black whatever the colour of the dog.

Size

Ideal height measured at the withers 14 inches (35–36 cm) for bitches, 14½ inches (37 cm) for dogs. Anything more than one inch above these heights to be considered a serious fault.

Faults

Domed or receding skull; lack of stop; large, drooping or pricked ears; overdeveloped cheeks; weak jaw; snipy muzzle; not full complement of teeth; crooked forelegs, cow hocks; tail kinked, short or carried over back; white or white colour predominating; pink or flesh coloured nose; blue eyes in any other colour than merles; nervousness; full or light eye; under- or overshot mouth.

Anyone reading these Standards will have noticed how the size has changed over the years, starting at 12 inches (30–31 cm) and now up to 14 inches (35–36 cm) ideal for bitches, 14½ inches (37 cm) for dogs. People sometimes ask if there is a height disqualification. There is not in this country although the U.S.A. has one; dogs can be measured in the ring and turned out if they are over 16 inches (40–41 cm). In this country the Kennel Club will not recognise a height disqualification so it is left to the judges to keep a check on size. I think on the whole they do a pretty good job. You do sometimes get runs of big or small ones winning but, on the whole, size keeps within bounds with a slight upward bias.

It is easy to breed a good big one but the breeder must keep a watch on size in his kennel as it is a most insidious thing and creeps up and up. One of the great advantages of Shelties is that they can be picked up and carried if necessary; also they can follow a bicycle or horse and walk all day.

Another important point in the Standard are the words 'lithe and active'. Looking up lithe in the *Oxford Dictionary*, it says 'Pliant, supple, bending and twisting and turning easily.' Now, to do this, a Sheltie must be well-made and balanced. I am afraid a lot of the dogs seen in the show ring today have trouble even getting out of the way of their own feet!

It must always be remembered that the Sheltie is a working breed and not a fireside ornament. Freedom of movement is essential.

There are the following Shetland Sheepdog Clubs: the English Shetland Sheepdog Club, the largest; it has several sections in different parts of the country. The Scottish Shetland Sheepdog Club; the Northern Counties Shetland Sheepdog Club; the Mid-Western Shetland Sheepdog Club; the Shetland Sheepdog Club of Wales, the Shetland Island Sheepdog Club and the Yorkshire Shetland Sheepdog Club.

I have not given the secretaries names and addresses as they do change and I know a great deal of trouble and unhappiness was caused by Miss D. Currie's name and address being left in one Sheltie book after she had died. If you want a secretary's name write to the Kennel Club at 1 Clarges Street, Piccadilly, London, W.1.

3   Your First Sheltie

Reasons for having a Sheltie

To start with, the Sheltie is such an affectionate and biddable dog, a handy size for the modern house. They have lived with man for a very long time so it is essential for their own peace of mind that they live as one of the family. They are not dogs to keep in large numbers where it is impossible to give them the love and attention they need.

Shelties are a very intelligent breed; they learn extremely quickly, they seem to sense what you want them to do; in fact, some of them seem to have a built in radar that lets them know when their master or mistress is within a few miles of home. It is nothing to do with hearing as my dog who had this sense very highly developed was stone deaf in the latter part of her life but it did not stop her knowing when I was nearing home, whether I had been away a few hours, days or weeks. Other people have told me the same thing about their 'special' dogs.

Another attraction of the Sheltie is their infinite variety of colour. There is something to suit everybody: sable starting at pale cream or what is called wheaten in Cairn Terriers; wolf sable which has a cream undercoat with black shadings, not a very attractive colour as it has a curious steely look about it. Then there is rich clear gold and red gold, these colours shaded with black, and then the really rich shaded sables, a dark mahogany with black tips. Tricolours are black with tan markings on face and legs, with various coloured tan markings, pale cream down to rich red. Then there are black and whites, which are like the tricolours without the tan markings and are called bi-colours in America, and unless they have a fair amount of white they are rather dreary.

Lastly come the blue merles; this is not an original Sheltie colour as they are unknown on the Islands. To get this colour, a tricolour Sheltie must have been mated to a blue merle Collie. Of course the colour has been in the breed for so long now that the Collie blood must have got very thin, but merles do tend to run to size. It is a very difficult colour as you get all shades of blue — some sandy, dirty mud and lavender, all of which are wrong; the operative word is blue. They are not a colour for novices to dabble in as they can be heart-breaking. Bad ones can be very ugly and difficult to sell.

In this colour, eyes can be blue or brown or a mixture of both. All other colours want to have dark brown eyes. Every colour can have full white Collie markings, i.e. white collar and front, legs and tip of tail, and a white blaze up the face is permissible though not so popular in the show ring as a whole coloured face.

You cannot show sable merles. This is a mixture of the different coloured sables instead of blue.

Then there are the ones called mismarks; dogs which have more white than colour, just sable or tricolour heads and patches on the body. They are often rather attractive to look at and sell well as pets. A lot of the original dogs were marked like this and it is nothing to be ashamed of if you breed one.

If you want an aggressive dog that catches and kills, do not get a Sheltie. I have known one which walked about with six mouse tails hanging out of its mouth and then gave a cough and out came the mice and ran away! You do get the exception to prove the rule but don't expect your Sheltie to kill things. They enjoy a chase across a field after a rabbit but unless encouraged soon give up and come back to you.

This makes taking them for walks in the country very troublefree as they seem to know they must not run sheep but will skirt round the outside of the flock. They love to help herd chickens and, in the same way, they like to keep members of their family together when out for a walk.

In their personal habits they are rather like cats and will sit licking and cleaning their legs and feet after a walk. You will never find a Sheltie with dirty feet.

Once a Sheltie owner, always a Sheltie owner. Another good point from a pet owner's point of view is that they are so long-lived. Twelve to sixteen years is the usual.

Do not expect your Sheltie to greet everybody as a long lost friend. It is not a sheepdog characteristic to love everybody. It is their own family that has all their affection and they are often very suspicious of strangers and resent being petted by them. It is this characteristic that has given them the reputation of being shy, but I do not call a dog shy because it doesn't welcome attentions from perfect strangers and prefers to remain untouched by strange hands. It can be rather a bore when showing them and you may have to take trouble making them realise you want the judge to touch them.

Another point that makes them such nice house dogs is the way they can efface themselves in a room and you would not know a dog was there. They are the most unrestless dogs and will not stir for hours on end, but let someone ring the door bell and they are up in arms at once.

If you have children, get your Sheltie young too. Like that, they will grow up together and become the greatest pals. But an older dog will often be difficult with young children.

The Sheltie as a Pet

When you decide you want a Sheltie pup as a pet, do go to a reputable breeder. Shun a kennel that advertises a lot of different breeds. This is a sure sign of a dealer and the pup you get will most likely have come from the wilds of Wales or Scotland at an early age with the chance of having picked up some infection on the way.

The most satisfactory place from which to get a pet puppy is the small kennel where the dogs live in the house and are pets, and the puppies are reared in the kitchen so get used to noises, are played with and are spoken to a lot. Small puppies want a lot of handling when young. You can always tell if they have been by the way they feel when you pick them up. If they go all stiff and hard you may be sure they have not been handled. It doesn't say that they won't respond to love and affection when you have got them but it is easier to start off with one that is already trusting.

Shelties as a breed are inclined to be hand shy. That is one of the reasons why it is important to get them young. Eight or nine weeks is best. Earlier than that they can be a lot of trouble unless you are used to dealing with young puppies.

Riverhill Rather Smart.

If there are young children in the house you must see the puppy does not get too much playing with. A young puppy needs a great deal of sleep.

If you are wanting a show puppy then you want an older one as it is easier to tell how they are going to develop. But when it is a question of just a pet, then eight or nine weeks is the right time to start them off in their new home.

You want to get a feeding chart from the breeder with the right amounts of food to give. I have said elsewhere how easy it is to overfeed puppies. When they have come away from the rest of the litter they miss the competition. It sometimes helps to put your fingers into the dish and push against the pup's head, stimulating competition.

Always remember that whoever looks after the puppy and feeds it the first few days will, willy nilly, become its master or mistress. I have known cases where a puppy has been bought for a child who is at school and although the child has come home only a few days after the puppy's arrival it has already attached itself to the mother and will have little to do with its intended owner.

If you can afford it and have the room get two, but mind they are the same sex. They will amuse each other when left alone and keep each other warm at night. Two will take much more exercise with each other and save you having to walk so far.

There are some golden rules about house training. First and foremost, always put the pup outside the moment it has had its meal and when it wakes up after a sleep. Put it out in the same place so it gets the idea that that is the place to relieve itself. Always praise it when it does and make it feel it's been clever.

A young pup can't go all night without relieving itself so put down some newspaper in a corner on a rubber mat or piece of linoleum. It is no good scolding a young puppy if it does make a puddle. It is different when it is older and if it is still dirty, but as a general rule Shelties are naturally very clean and they always want to please so if you praise them when they are good they will soon get the idea. The great moment is when they come and ask to go out. Then you know your troubles are over. Always remember intelligent anticipation is the keynote of successful house training.

It is advisable to get your puppy used to a collar and lead at an early age. Shelties have a natural antipathy to something round their necks so put a small thin collar on at ten weeks or so, leave it on and it will bed down into the coat. When the pup ignores it then attach a thin lead or thick piece of string, let the pup drag it about, then take hold of the other end. You may find you are playing a fish, to the accompaniment of screams and roars, or the pup may take it quite quietly and after a jump or two lead along like an old hand.

Very often the ones who make a great deal of fuss the first few minutes give in very quickly and the ones who do not make much fuss just
go stubborn, stick their toes in and have to be dragged along. This may
go on for days. It sometimes helps if you have another dog to lead it
along too and the pup may follow. Once they have got the idea, your
troubles are over as Shelties hate being pulled by the neck and they will
trot along on a loose lead.

Remember, no walks outside the garden till they have had their innoc-
ulations as young puppies are very vulnerable, and no long walks till
they are at least six months and their bones have knit up properly.

Shelties learn their names very quickly. The best thing is to say the
name over and over again with a bit of biscuit in your hand and when
the pup comes up to you say the name and hand him a piece. You won't
have to do this often before the pup will come at once the moment you
say its name.

It is also important to get the pup used to having its mouth opened
and, in fact, to have all his head handled. If at any time he has to be
given a pill or a dose and you can open his mouth without a fuss half
the battle is over.

You also want to get him used to being brushed and combed. Look
at his feet and cut his nails if necessary. If all this is done when he is
young you won't have a full size battle on your hands which might
happen if you wait till he is adult.

Remember teething is rather a tricky time. Very often it makes
puppies feel ill. Their mouths get sore and they may go off their food.
You want to watch out and see the teeth are coming out and not im-
peding the second ones. This particularly applies to the canines, the four
large teeth. If the second ones come through and the milk ones are still
in place, so that there is no room for the big canines, you want to go to
your veterinary surgeon and have him remove the milk canines under a
general anaesthetic. They must be disected out, otherwise they may
break off and you are back at square one and no better off. If you don't
have anything done, your dog's mouth may be ruined as the canines, not
having room to come down in the right position, will get distorted and
shoot out sideways. If your vet is not used to Shelties he may say, 'Oh,
leave them, they will come out by themselves.' But they will not, so
don't take *no* for an answer.

The first teeth start coming out at about four months. The little
incisors move first and the canines are always the last to move. By six
months they should have all but a few of the very back ones.

Ears are another thing that may want some help to stay in the right
position. They tend to go up prick. If you don't mind this, well and good
and you needn't bother, but if you like them tipped over you may have
to help matters along.

When a puppy is teething the ears may either go up or down. If down, it does not matter as they will come up later. If they don't you can cut a little of the hair off the base to help them rise.

The prick ones are the ones that cause the trouble. It is really a matter of perseverance. Leather oil (liquid dubbin) is the answer: a drop on the ball of the thumb rubbed up the inside of the ear. You can feel a ligament that runs from the base of the ear to nearly the tip. Rub the oil into this. If you can do it two or three times a day so much the better. Never put a lot on at a time as you want to rub it all in. The oil has a spirit base so it is possible to do this. You can also rub a little on to the outside of the tip of the ear. This should do the trick if you start the moment the ear goes prick. If it does not, you want to put a dab of Kaolin poultice on the inside of the ear tip, dry it off with ashes or talc powder. By the time it has worn off the ear should have set in the right position, but remember it is no good just doing it once or twice and then leaving it.

Do not, I repeat, *do not,* put a heavy weight on the tip. As likely as not it will make the ear go over backwards and that is the last thing you want to happen. The secret is to keep the ear supple and soft.

When teething is over, the ears should settle permanently. Sometimes, bitches' ears will go up when they are in season and dogs' when they

Ch. Rhinog Waltzing Matilda and her son, Ch. Rhinog Hunky Dory.

mate a bitch, but they usually come over naturally when these excitements are over.

It is a good thing for the pup to have his own bed where he can take his toys and guard his bones. If possible a wooden box or one of the canvas beds are best. Baskets are real flea traps and also get chewed to bits. There are some very good composite beds made but get one with a rough surface. Dogs hate to slip about in their beds and some of these composite beds are very smooth and slippery. A piece of old carpet cut to fit the bed makes good bedclothes. It can be easily shaken or washed out.

You should always feed your pup in the same place. Dogs are great creatures of habit so it is up to you to see he gets into good ones. Do not give him rubber toys as they can be dangerous. You can get raw hide chews which they love and give them endless amusement and do no harm.

Now to the question of discipline. Shelties are intelligent and want to please. Of course, you get the odd wayward one but the general run want to do what you want, so begin as you mean to go on. Don't laugh at them one minute and scold them the next for doing the same thing.

Ch. Parrock's Possibility and her sire, Ch. Scylla Vaguely Blue. They gained their titles on the same day having won under the same three judges.

You will just confuse them. They are easily taught 'no' just by your tone of voice but if they really do something that wants a smack, a rolled up newspaper is the thing to use. It makes a lot of noise when you smack them and can't possibly do any harm.

The only occasions when they really need hurting is if they chase chickens or run sheep. That must be stamped on at once in no uncertain manner. If you cannot make them come up to you when you call, a clothes line attached to their collar is a useful tip. Do this and then take them where there are sheep or chickens and it is easy to catch them. As a rule they seem to know they mustn't run sheep but there is always the exception to prove the rule.

Another thing that wants controlling is barking. It is all right that they should bark if the front door bell rings but a dog that goes on barking when a stranger comes into the house and you are there is a perfect nuisance and it wants stopping. Given any encouragement at all Shelties will bark and go on barking, so see that they know you do not like it from an early age or it will get out of hand. What is funny in a little pup isn't in a grown dog and always remember your voice and the tone you use is your most effective instrument of control.

4   Breeding Shelties

Picking Breeding Stock

Having made up your mind that you want to breed Shelties, it is a case of making haste slowly. Do not rush out and buy from all and sundry. You should go to as many shows as possible to watch the dogs and see which of the winners you like the look of. Get in touch with their owners, but never before the judging when everybody is very busy and rather het up till they have been judged. Afterwards is a different matter and owners will be glad to help you.

My advice is: if you can find someone willing to sell you a young bitch with a good pedigree who has done some winning, strain every nerve to get her. You will probably have to pay a good price but it is worth it. If you fail to get what you want, try for a good young puppy from a bitch who has already produced winners. The E.S.S.C. charts of families can be of great help here. You may have to put your name down and wait, but a puppy from a strain of good mothers who produce winners is worth waiting for.

You may be able to get a well-bred bitch on breeding terms from one of the good kennels. You do not want one that is a throw out and the owners think it is the only way to get quit of her. Here again, the breeding behind is all important. Remember that grandparents play a very large part in the puppies' make up. Have something in writing about the terms; what, for instance, happens if there are only one or two puppies, who pays the stud fee and how many puppies you have to give back. The usual is some cash, £20 to £60, and first and second pick from the first litter with a proviso that if there are only two puppies one should go from the second litter. Do not accept terms where you have to give up puppies from several litters and play fair by the bitch's owner. Do not suddenly say you are not going to breed from her after all.

Always consult the breeder of your bitches on who to mate them to, anyhow for the first time. When you are more experienced you can launch out on your own and prove your own theories.

Do not get bitches that have totally different pedigrees. Get ones that have some names in common.

I am not an advocate of close breeding as there are so few dogs good enough to inbreed to. Always remember that when you inbreed you are doing so to the bad points as well as the good. I have seen kennels that have stamped their stock with maybe good heads or coats but also straight shoulders or round eyes. The genetic theorists may say if you do so and so, such and such will happen, but in practice something quite different turns up. Shelties in particular have not 'read the book'. If they can flummox you they will.

Here are just a few examples of what they can do: you mate two sables together and get a litter of black and whites, a colour that is supposed to be recessive; mating a merle to a tri and getting five tri pups, repeating the mating and getting five merles; having a small, very heavy-coated champion with perfect ears who never sired anything but huge flat-coated ones with either low or prick ears.

We have a greatly prized aid to help in the picking of sires to suit our bitches. It is a split pedigree book. They are made for racehorse breeders and can be got from a stationer in Newmarket. They are not cheap but are well worth every penny. It is fascinating fitting pedigrees together and seeing which ones you think make the best pattern.

If you are thinking of having a kennel affix, which is a must for a serious breeder, choose one that is easy to say. People can be put off by a name they do not know how to pronounce. Some breeders give their dogs Gaelic names which may look nice but are difficult to spell and are the very devil to pronounce. Actually Gaelic names are wrong for Shelties. Pick an affix that looks nice in writing as well as being easy to pronounce.

Ch. Riverhill Rare Gold with her four daughters; Ch. R. Ready Cash (1958), Ch. R. Real Gold (1956), Ch. R. Rather Rich (1959) and Ch. R. Rarity of Glenmist (1961).

Glancing down the list of C.C. winners one is struck by how attractive some of these affixes look: Ashbank, Clerwood, Exford, Greenscrees, Glenhill, Hazelhead, Helensdale, Whytelaw, Wyndora, Wansdyke — all country-sounding names and suitable for a working breed.

When you have got your affix, start with some method in your naming, i.e. if the affix begins with say R you can have all the dogs' names beginning with R, like the Riverhill Rufus, or you can have a different letter for each litter. Do not use up all your best names in your first few litters as it is sickening to waste a really good name on a puppy that turns out to be only a pet.

Keeping Records

If you are going to take your breeding seriously you must keep records, the more the better. To start with, you want a stud book with your dog's

All the children of Ch. Riverhill Rather Rich: Ch. R. Richman (1968), Ch. R. Rather Dark, a third generation champion bitch (1965), Ch. R. Raider (1965) and Ch. R. Rather Nice, a third generation champion bitch (1963).

Ch. Spark (1958), Ch. Shan Tung (1960), Ch. Sweet Sultan (1957), Ch. Midas (1956) and Ch. Spice (1960).

name, pedigree and, if a bitch, a column for when mated and the result. Then it is a good thing to keep a copy of the pedigree of every litter you breed. You can get books of pedigree forms for this and write the number, sex and colour of the litter and the registered names if any are registered. We have done this ever since we started breeding and it is now quite a library and has been of inestimable value over the years.

Another good thing to do is weigh the puppies every week till they are ten weeks. Sunday is a good day to pick to do this as it is easy to remember. I wish we had done it earlier but we only started a year or two ago and already I can see it is going to be a most useful guide as to the puppies' eventual size.

Three other books are worth keeping; one for the name and address of people who buy your puppies and the puppies' names, so that, when they write to you years later and say they would like another just like 'Lassie' who has died you can look up and see what puppy they had. Secondly, you should keep a book with your dogs' show records. They are difficult to remember if they are not written down. If you don't,

sure as fate you will enter your dog in classes for which he is ineligible and nothing is more discouraging than getting disqualified and having to return the card and prize money and pay a fine as well.

It is interesting, too, to have a photograph of each dog to put in your stud book. I love to look in ours; it brings back so many happy memories and you can see how your present day dogs have improved, at least I hope you can.

Last but not least, keep a book with suitable names. Then when you use one put the date against the name and you will be able to trace the dog years later or if you want to use the name again you can see if the specified ten years are up and it is available again.

Ch. Shahreen (1968), Ch. Streak Lightning (1970), Ch. Such a Spree (1970), Ch. Such a Beano (1971), Ch. Special Edition (1966) and their sire, Strikin' Midnight at Shelert.

5   Whelping and Weaning

Whelping

Having got your bitch safely mated to the dog of your choice, let her go on leading a normal life with plenty of exercise right up to a few days before she is due to whelp. The official time is sixty-three days from mating but we find Shelties very rarely go as long as this, sixty to sixty-two being more normal. Between the third and fourth week of her pregnancy she may go off her food for a day or two; don't worry, it is a good sign. On the other hand, if she continues to eat normally it does not mean she has missed.

It you are very anxious to know if she is in whelp, the third week is the time to let a veterinary surgeon, who is skilled in small animal work, feel her. Personally, I would rather rely on my own observations as her general behaviour will usually tell you. Our vet says he will never pronounce on a Sheltie — they have made a fool of him too often. The puppies are sometimes carried very high and only come back a few days before whelping. Her meat should be increased after the fourth week and it is better that she should have two small meals rather than one large one.

Now to whelping boxes. We find the large size tea chest ideal. Lay it on its side, cut out the top side, make a loose lid to fit over it, then you can lift it off to look inside and see the puppies without having to go down on your knees. Fix a hinged board across the front, high enough to keep the puppies in but not too high to stop the bitch from getting in easily. This board can be let down when the puppies reach the age when they want to come out to relieve themselves and it makes a ramp for them to crawl up into the box.

Some people prefer open whelping boxes but you will notice that if a bitch is left to herself she will go off and dig a hole under a shed or burrow about under a chair or settee; her instinct is to get into the dark. Other points in favour of the tea chest, besides making a nice dark cave, are that it is draught-proof and also the firm sides make something for the bitch to press against when she is straining.

We always use newspaper as bedding. The bitch will scratch and tear it up into little bits and pack it into the corners of the box. We keep on adding papers till she has a nice deep bed.

When she finishes whelping, the paper can be cleared out and she can go on a heavy wheat or flour sack; this gives a very good surface for the pups to get a grip on whilst sucking. I hate to see small puppies on a smooth surface trying to feed when their little hind legs are slipping away all the time. These heavy sacks are rather hard to come by but if you are lucky enough to have a baker who bakes his own bread, you may be able to persuade him to sell you some. They will want washing out but once you have got them they will last for years and should the bitch be a bed scraper, all you need do is put a piece of hardboard just smaller than the bed floor inside the sack and it will put a stop to it.

If you cannot get sacks, bits of stair carpet will do instead, but they are harder to keep flat and it is essential to have something that will not ruck up, is easy to wash, and not slippery.

There is now some good man-made fibre bedding on the market: Vetbed and Wertex are two of these. I use Vetbed for the first few weeks after the bitch has whelped and find it very satisfactory, but when the puppies are old enough to go out into the kennel they bring sawdust into the bed which is very difficult to get out of the bedding. For this reasons I revert to the sacks since these can be easily shaken clean.

When whelping is going to start, the usual signs are general uneasiness, a lot of panting and scratching about in the bed; the bitch constantly turns, looks at her flanks and licks her vagina. When she really starts straining in earnest, you may expect the first puppy to arrive in an hour or two.

Shelties are easy whelpers and very good mothers; of course, you get the odd one that is troublesome and with a first litter, we like to be there as the bitch may not get the first puppy out of the bag in time to stop it suffocating but once the first one has arrived safely she is best left alone. Your being there may distract her and she has a lot to do; cleaning up, cutting the cord, eating the afterbirth — it is very important that she does this as it helps to sustain her for the next few hours. We like to put a hot water bottle in the corner of the box so that the first born puppies have something warm to nestle against while the others are arriving.

Some bitches have a lot of water and the puppies keep on getting wet every time a new one is born so it is a good thing to have a rough towel handy to give them a rub when necessary. Puppies usually come at half-hour intervals but after two or three there may be quite a long gap before the rest of the litter arrives.

When you think they have all been born, clean out the bed and put the bitch and puppies on a nice clean sack; they should be sucking and she should be giving them all a good licking. An egg well-beaten up in a little milk can be given to her and then the quieter she is kept, the better.

The room or shed where she is should be kept at between 60 and 70 degrees for at least the first ten days. It is a good thing to have a thermometer in the room. Remember, the puppies have come from a very hot place and it is important they should not get chilled or they may get pneumonia and fade away in a day or two. When I hear about lost litters, I always wonder about the conditions in which the puppies were whelped. I am sure more puppies are lost through cold than any other reason and even if the pups do not die, their food goes to keeping them warm rather than on helping them to grow.

In forty-eight years of breeding, we have only lost ten whole litters; of them, two had outside infections, two were singletons and five Caesarians. Of course you get the odd puppy dying and sometimes one is born dead, usually the first or last born.

Bitches are always very clean when they have puppies so it is a good thing to let your bitch out to relieve herself once the puppies are born.

Ch. Riverhill Rather Special and her two puppies, both of them winners in 1979.

No solid food should be given till she has had an action of the bowels; if this has not happened in the first thirty-six hours, you should give her a dessertspoonful of Milk of Magnesia. This should do the trick and then she can have solid food; raw meat is best.

Keep an eye on the milk glands for the first few days. The puppies tend to leave the top ones and these may get rather swollen, but unless they become really sore, leave them alone and they will right themselves. If you feel you must do something, draw off a little of the milk by hand.

If you are going to have the dew-claws off, it should be done on the fourth or fifth day. Should there be back ones, they must come off, but opinions differ about the front ones. We usually take them off as they can get badly torn if the dog runs about on rough ground. It is best to let a vet do this unless you have a steady hand, but a thing you must do yourself is cut the puppies' toe nails every week after they are ten days-old. This is quite easy to do with a pair of strong nail scissors and, later, when the puppies get older and the nails harder, a pair of nail clippers. If this isn't done, you will find your bitch refusing to feed her puppies unless you hold her, as puppies' claws get as sharp as kittens and will scratch and tear her teats.

To sum up, here are the important points. One; see the bitch has plenty of exercise up to a few days before whelping. Two; see the shed or room where she whelps is 60—70 degrees and stays that way for at least ten days. Three; have the puppies bedded on something they can get a grip on. Four; no solid food till the bitch has had an action of the bowels. Five; cut the puppies' claws every week after they are ten days old. Six; if you have an infra red lamp, do not put it over the top of the bed; let it shine on the ground in front of the box. Seven; keep the bitch and puppies very quiet for the first week.

One last word, do not fuss; if you do, you may agitate the bitch and distract her attention from her puppies, and finally, if you are not happy about anything, call in your veterinary surgeon. It is better to be safe than sorry.

Weaning

It is impossible to be dictatorial about when to start weaning; it all depends on the dam and the quality of the milk she has but on an average three weeks is the time to start or when the pups start nosing about and licking one's fingers.

Everybody has his own ideas on what is the best milk food to start on. All the baby milk foods are good but expensive. We use Carnation Full Cream Milk diluted half and half with hot water with a little honey added. We find this very easy to prepare, the pups like it and we get no scours. Start with a dessertspoonful. We use an enamel saucer from a doll's tea set. This is just the size to hold under a puppy's nose and I would not be without it for anything. Lay a towel on top of the tea chest, pick each pup out in turn, put them on the towel and hold the saucer under their nose. If they take no notice put a little pressure on the top of the head till the nose touches the milk. Once they get a taste on their tongue they will start lapping, even if they blow a few bubbles in the process.

The milk should be blood heat to start with, but be careful not to feed it too hot. Nothing upsets puppies quicker.

After two or three days increase the amount to two dessertspoonfuls. After a week, add a little Farex and feed one scraped raw meat meal; half an ounce is plenty to start with. You may have to put the first few bits into their mouths but once they have the taste there is no holding them.

At about five weeks we stop feeding the milk meal separately. Put it in a dish and watch that one pup doesn't hog the lot. Meat we always feed separately. At this time we give the dam a dish of cornflakes and milk with honey added last thing and the pups soon learn to come out and have some too.

If the bitch's milk dries up at five weeks, which it does sometimes, you will have to increase the feeds. Start adding a little fine puppy meal to the milk and Farex feed, with half an ounce of raw meat for lunch, the same for tea; and last thing, cornflakes in cows' milk with a teaspoon of honey added. If the puppies scour at all, cut down on the bulky food. Shelties do not have a very large capacity and nothing upsets them quicker than overfeeding.

At six weeks the puppies should be independant and the dam sleeping away. She will want to go and look at her puppies and perhaps have a game but don't let them suck. If she's got anything, it won't be very nice and may upset them. During the last week or so before they are weaned keep her away from the puppies when she has been fed or she will go straight and bring up her food for them. Watch out for this. She may start earlier and a large lump of meat can get stuck in a pup's throat and choke it. The better the mother, the more she will do it. We had one bitch who had only to hear any puppy crying to rush and regurgitate what ever she had eaten last.

It is best to worm the pups just before they are weaned, at about five weeks. For some reason, the first litters always seem to be much worse in this respect than later ones. Get pills from your vet and follow the instruction carefully. Do one puppy at a time, then you will see if the pill has worked. If you dose them all at once you can't keep track. One pup may throw up its pill and so not get rid of its worms and you won't know which one it was.

At eight weeks, our puppies start having half a Canovel vitamin tablet, increased to one whole one when they weigh 10 lbs. There are several good additives. You can consult your veterinary surgeon to see which one he recommends. We find Canovel good to start on and the puppies soon get to eat them like sweets. They are also very good for old dogs too. Puppies need something while they are growing and particularly while they are teething. This seems to put a great drain on their system. We have found Stress very good.

Always remember that the bones in the legs don't really knit up till they are six months. That's why too much exercise is out until they are that age. Jumping onto chairs and going up and down stairs should be discouraged if you want your puppy to have a nice pair of straight front legs and strong hocks.

It must be remembered that this is only a rough guide and much depends on the bitch. You may have to start feeding at ten days or not until the puppies are nearly five weeks if the bitch has a lot of rich milk the puppies won't bother to eat themselves and you may have to start straight on to scraped raw meat as that may appeal to them and you must try and help relieve the bitch or she will get very pulled down.

We carry on with four meals a day till the puppies are three months; then we combine both meat meals together in the evening at about six o'clock. At six weeks, we leave off the Farex and only feed fine puppy meal soaked overnight in cows' milk. Make the change over gradually so that they get used to the taste. Keep on with the honey.

General Feeding

At six months, when they have teethed, we cut out the last meal of cornflakes and milk and then they are on two meals: a small breakfast of puppy meal and milk, and an evening meal of six to seven ounces of meat. When adult, they have eight ounces if they can take it but we find different dogs vary considerably on how much meat they can stand. All the dogs get their meat weighed individually and one family we have can never take more than seven ounces except when in whelp. The stud dogs get nine to ten ounces.

I believe in a mixed diet for dogs and we ring the changes between paunch, raw meat, raw mince, some butchers' and some pet foods, tinned meat, lights and all offals, and once a week a soaked biscuit meal with meat scraps added. They have seaweed powder on their food once a week and a small handful of dry biscuit to go to bed with.

It must be remembered that Shelties aren't big eaters. You get the exception to prove the rule but give the average Sheltie too much soaked food and they will get upset tummies or eczema or become bilious.

There is one point I should like to make, and that is: touch and handle your puppies from a few days old and when their eyes and ears open talk to them. Quite a lot of research has been done on this and it is found that eight days till eight weeks is the vital time for them to get used to being handled. If you feed them one by one that helps but do talk to them as well.

6 Kennel Management

Stud Dogs

On the whole, Shelties are very unsexy so starting a young dog on his stud career may take a good deal of patience and understanding. Let him start with an older bitch who has had litters, is flirtatious and will encourage him. On no account let him start with a maiden. Eleven or twelve months is the right age to let a dog have his first bitch.

To start with he will not want you to hold the bitch and it is best to stand quietly by and only get hold of the bitch when he has mounted her and tied, then you can help him to turn. When he has mated several bitches he won't mind you holding the bitch and you can help matters by holding her tail out of the way with one hand while keeping the other under her between her hind legs. In this way you can feel if the dog is the right height to effect a mating easily. If he is too low you can raise him on a board or a mat. We have several boards of varying thicknesses. It saves a lot of time and wasted energy if the dog is just the right height to enter the bitch without straining.

We always teach our stud dogs to mate on a strong carpenter's bench. It is much easier to control a fractious bitch if she is on a level with you. Also it is easier to hold them during the tie if you are standing up rather than down on your knees. The dogs soon get used to it and will stand waiting to be put up on the bench so that they can get on with the job.

You want to limit the number of bitches a young dog has at least till he is eighteen months old. I have known dogs ruined by over-use at an early age. Managed sympathetically, a stud dog can go on siring puppies for years. We have had them sire litters at twelve and thirteen years of age.

Stud dogs must be well fed with plenty of meat and kept in hard condition with plenty of exercise. It is essential that their hind-quarters are muscular and well developed. Dogs with weak hocks have trouble mounting a bitch and very little drive to achieve a tie.

Always remember that dogs are not machines and that they may take an instant dislike to a bitch for no apparent reason. Even if they are very experienced studs, they can refuse to have anything to do with her. If this happens you just have to accept it. Sometimes if you have another stud dog and bring him in it may make the first one think again.

Remember, too, that bitches have their own ideas on what they want. They may fight against one dog and welcome another. That's why it is always more satisfactory if the bitch's owner can come with her and see for themselves the situation as you cannot use another dog without consulting the bitch's owner.

We had one bitch sent to our keenest stud dog who utterly refused to take the slightest notice of her. We rang the owners and they asked us to send her elsewhere, which we did. She was mated and had a litter. The next time they brought her themselves as I think they thought we hadn't really tried, but exactly the same thing happened again and they saw for themselves he just was not interested in that particular bitch. And this was a dog who mated his first bitch at nine months and his last in his fourteenth year.

Never let a dog mate two bitches in a day, even if he will try. I know some Terrier breeds do this but if you want your dog to stay fertile I do not advise it. For some reason, everybody's bitches seem to come on heat at the same time and it is tempting to over-use your dog but, if you have his good at heart, don't. Dogs, wolves and foxes are, I believe, the only animals to have a tie; but they can sire puppies with a slip

Ch. Midnitesun Justin Time, a Working Group winner.

mating, in and out. The usual tie can be from five minutes to two hours. We have found that ties of an hour or over usually do not produce puppies. Young dogs sometimes don't tie till they have mated one or two bitches and the older a dog gets the longer he ties.

Runs and Kennels

How ever few dogs you have, you must have at least two runs. One so you can shut in the adults when you are tired of having them under your feet in the house and where they will be safe and not escape into the road because someone has left the garden gate open; a second one for the puppies which should be in two parts if possible, half paved and the other half grass. Keep the grass cut short as it makes cleaning up so much easier. You do not want the ground to become fouled.

Of course, if you have several dogs and breed a lot of litters you will want at least two puppy runs as you cannot put the young puppies with older ones, and equally the older pups with the adult dogs.

You can buy very good sectional puppy runs, 6 feet by 4 feet (approx. 180 cm by 120 cm). They are not cheap but being strong and well galvanized will last for years. It is very handy being able to move them about and make the run what size and shape you want.

When we moved at the end of the war we were determined to have one large paved run, having had a concrete one which used to crack when there was a severe frost and have to be patched. We decided to have concrete paving stones, then if one cracks it can be removed quite easily and a new one put in. There are two sizes, 4 feet by 2 feet (approx. 120 cm by 60 cm) and 2 feet square (61 cm square). They are best laid on sand but not cemented together. If this is done the run may turn into a swimming bath after heavy rain, but if they are just laid edge to edge the water drains off in no time at all. You do get a problem of weeds coming up in the cracks but this can easily be dealt with by spraying them with Weedex in the spring when they should keep clean for at least six months. The 2 feet square stones make splendid hard paths between the runs and kennels. In Great Britain, you get such a lot of rain, and consequently mud, that being able to go dry and clean-footed about your business is a godsend.

Another thing I can highly recommend is growing ivy up the chain link fencing. It makes a most splendid wind break, looks nice, stops the dogs looking out and barking at all and sundry, is easily kept tidy as it needs the minimum of cutting and does not shed needles or prickly leaves. It also makes the fencing look very strong and discourages dogs trying to get out.

It has often struck me what a lot of unnecessary discomfort dog breeders put up with both on their own account and their dogs. How often one has been stung on the legs by nettles when going through a gate into a run or seen large patches of them in the run itself and round the kennels. Even if they are cut off they leave nasty stiff stalks which no dog would run over, and nettles increase by leaps and bounds every year till before you know where you are half the run is a nettle bed. This painful and unsightly condition can soon be dealt with if you take a little trouble.

The answer is Sodium Chlorate. I can hear people saying 'Poison! I couldn't use that in my dog runs.' Take it from me, this is nonsense. I have helped clear a farm completely of nettles, aided by a Solo Spray, buckets of water, tins of Sodium Chlorate crystals and a large wooden spoon to stir them with. As to poison, the dogs have drunk the mixture out of the pails before I could stop them but with no ill effects and cattle will come and graze round the dead nettle clumps with relish. The best time to spray is when the nettles are about a foot high. If the clumps are very old and strong they may need a second spraying. Do not let any of the spray get on a hedge or the leaves of any plant you do not want killed. It is best to spray on a windless day.

Thistles are another weed that can become a menace in grass runs. There is a sure way of getting rid of them, too, and that is by constant cutting or mowing but it is best done when the moon is waxing. I know this sounds like an old wives' tale. We thought so when we were told about it but the proof of the pudding is in the eating. Our runs were full of thistle when we first came here so we thought we would try it out and did our cutting when the moon was waxing. The following year we could hardly believe our eyes; only a few stragglers came up and they were soon dealt with. The place is now clear of thistles so don't laugh, just try it and see what happens.

Lots of people keep two or three dogs together in one kennel but we have never found it satisfactory. One dog always becomes the master and bullies. You cannot let them have bones to go to bed with for the same reason. Talking of bones, we bed on straw, never woodwool, as we lost a dog with peritonitis from eating a bone on woodwool. It pierced the bowel and when the vet realised what was happening peritonitis had set in and gone too far.

We have wooden kennels fully lined but not with asbestos sheeting as that sweats so. I like wooden floors for dogs and we paint them with bitumastic paint and have sawdust in a corner. All the beds and tea chests are painted too but do not use paint with any lead in it.

I am not a great believer in endless scrubbing out of kennels. I think the enusing damp does more harm than the chance of some infection from dirt. The only kennels of ours that get scrubbed out are the whelping ones and the puppies' kennels if they get very messy.

Have your kennels high enough to stand up in. Creeping about doubled up in a kennel is a sure way to get lumbago. We have one large kennel with six divisions. The dogs can see each other but cannot bully. The stud dogs live in a different shed and have solid partitions. Then there are two separate kennels where the 'loners' live. There are always some dogs that perfer to live alone, out of sight of the others. I can sympathise with them. Dogs get very attached to their own kennels so try to put them where they will stay. It always amuses me when cleaning the kennels that the owner will come and stand by when it is being done to see that you are doing it right, and woebetide if another one comes and pokes his nose in.

We have three whelping kennels, well lined and warmed and not in general use. The bitches know what is going to happen when they are put in them and never mind vacating their normal home.

There are also three puppy kennels, all with clear glass lights about four inches from the ground. This enables the puppies to look out with their ears in the correct position. The last thing you want is for puppies to sit gazing up into the sky with ears falling into the prick position. This really applies to the adults too. We try and have windows they can look out of without a lot of head raising.

It pays to get an expert to install electricity in your sheds and kennels as you must have lights and be able to have infra red lamps in the whelping and puppy kennels, also a floodlight or two over the whole set up. Nothing is worse than floundering about in the dark with a torch in which the battery always seems to be giving out. If you can, have a solid shed where you can have an infra red fire as well as lamps. You can shut the dogs in together when wet to dry off. It saves hours of time and lots of dirty towels, but do get it installed by an expert. There have been so many terrible kennel fires caused by faulty wiring.

Night storage heaters are very handy to have in the dogs' kitchen or where the old pensioners sleep. Old dogs do seem to feel the cold so, we also have two large sheds just for use in wet or cold weather. These do not need to be lined.

We do not like having dogs shut all day in the kennels that they sleep in. I know this may sound pernickety but it does mean you have happy, healthy dogs who are not so bored they start kennel vices like coat chewing.

7   Grooming and Judging

Grooming

People often say to me, 'Don't Shelties' coats want an awful lot of attention to keep them looking nice?' And I always say, 'No, a brush once a week is ample except when they are shifting their coats; then a steel comb must be used to get the undercoat out.'

In the ordinary way you want to go easy with the comb. The only places where the coat may mat is behind the ears and down the fringes on the front legs and on the hind legs as far as the hocks, but normally a grooming with a brush of the Maison Pearson type, bristles not nylon, is all that is needed.

Once adult, the dogs will hold their coats for months and even years, then suddenly, oddly enough usually in the winter, they will have a grand moult and pounds of wool will come away. If you can find some-one to spin it for you it is well worth keeping as it is rather like Angora rabbit wool, very soft, a very pretty colour and, I am told, very hard wearing.

Bitches of course shift their coats more often, always about two months after they have been on heat, just at the time they would be whelping. If they have been mated you will notice the first place the coat comes away is on the belly and round the teats. This must be a pro-vision of nature so that the puppies will not have to compete with a mass of long hair when they want to feed. After rearing a litter the bitch has a complete moult and looks like a smooth dog. It takes nearly six months before she is in coat again.

It is always wise to keep an eye on toe nails as if the dog only runs on grass these may get over long and throw him back on his heels. The two centre toe nails tend to get longer than the outside ones and if this happens they want clipping back. The guillotine sort of clippers are best for the adult dog; they don't seem to squeeze the nails like ordinary clippers.

Then there is the question of bathing. Of course, if the dog has fleas or has been rolling in some filth they must be bathed but otherwise country dogs do not want a lot of washing. The time to do it is when they have had a moult and the coat is at rock bottom. Otherwise a full coated Sheltie is almost impossible to really wet down to the skin. I have seen one jump into a large pond, swim across, get out the far side, give one shake and be dry in a few minutes.

Before showing, of course, is rather a different matter, not that we do it very often and if you do make sure it is a day or two before the show as you want the coat to feel hard, not soft and glossy. The white parts can always do with a wash the night before a show. There is very little show preparation needed for a Sheltie. The hair on the hind legs from the hocks to the feet and the back of the pasterns on the front legs should be kept short. This should be done a few days before-hand.

Some dogs grow a great deal of hair on and around their ears. This wants sorting out, either with thinning scissors or with finger and thumb, but do not over do it or you will have the ears going up prick. How often I have heard a distraught exhibitor whose dogs ears are flying up in the ring say, 'They were so good but I thought I would tidy them up for the show.' If you are going to do it do it some days before the show, do not leave it till the night before. If you are lucky your show dog may have nice short smooth hair on its ears and you will not have to touch them.

Some people cut the whiskers off and the long eyebrow hairs. We used to do this but do not touch them now. It seemed to upset the dogs and after judging one day I decided I never noticed if they were on or off so it seemed pointless to go on doing it, especially as the dogs hated having it done.

When you know you are going to show your dog, it is a good thing to brush him as often as possible. Dip the brush in rain water and shake it over the dog, then brush the coat up towards the head all down the back. Rainwater to my mind is better than all the lotions and potions advertised and leaves the coat gleaming.

Before taking your dog into the ring give his white markings a good chalking. You can get chalk blocks to rub the legs with and powder to puff into his white front and ruff if he has one. Brush it out before you go into the show ring.

It is essential to teach your show dog to trot by your side on a loose lead. Any pulling or straining will effect his action and either make him cross his legs or prance. You want to have some titbit such as well-boiled liver in your pocket and teach him to look at your hand, with his ears raised. When he has stood in the correct position for the judge to look at him, give him a little piece. Shelties carry a penalty having to raise their ears and keep them up for the judge, as normally running at home the ears are folded back and only raised if their interest is aroused. This problem of ears is a great deterrent to them winning groups or Best in Show as very few are 'showing fools'. They easily get bored and then are overlooked.

The author judging.

Judging

There is a lot of nonsense written about judging and people being born with an eye and such like. Certainly judging seems to come easier to some but the chief thing about becoming a good judge is to know what you are looking for and to do this you must have a picture in your mind's eye of your ideal.

Besides integrity, which goes without saying, a judge must try to make his mind a complete blank as far as to who the dog is, who it belongs to, what it has won and how it is bred. You must look at every dog as if you had never seen it before. Try to be completely unbiased. I have heard judges say 'I can't see a blue merle' or 'I hate tris.' You are judging the dog as it stands; colour should not come into it except in the case of blue merles where 'blue' is the operative word. If the Standard just said merles like it says sables you could pass the bad coloured ones, but it says blue, then blue it should be and if the dog fails here it should be penalised.

One of the biggest failings in the modern Sheltie is bad shoulder angulation, not so much the actual shoulder blade but the upper arm which is so often too short and too straight. The upper arm is the bone from the lower point of the shoulder blade to the elbow. If this is wrong the dog may move straight coming towards you but when viewed from the side will be seen to hardly stretch out its leg at all and so be very restricted in its stride (see pages 27 and 28).

Sometimes people say 'I cannot see a straight shoulder.' A good tip is to look at the dog as if it were a horse and put a saddle on its back and you will see whether if he were a horse you would have a good long rein in your hands and if there would be plenty in front of the saddle. If he has, then the dog has a good shoulder.

People go mad about hereditary faults but seem to forget that straight shoulders are very hereditary and very difficult to get rid of once you have got them into your strain.

I think all judges should be made to study anatomy. After all, if judges did not put up badly constructed dogs breeders would have to pay attention to their dogs conformation and perhaps we should not hear such a lot about hip dysplasia and slipping patellas, etc.

To go back to judging, keep command of the ring. Do not let the exhibitors get into a huddle in a corner which they will do if given half a chance. When you have made up your mind pull out your winners into the centre of the ring and if possible keep them in the order you pull them out. It is very disheartening for an exhibitor to come out first and then be moved down the line to end up with only a reserve or V.H.C.

It is essential to keep a sense of proportion when judging. Do not go overboard about one thing, either a good point or equally a fault. Always remember that the Sheltie is a working breed and that if it has the most beautiful head and wonderful coat and has crooked front legs or upright shoulders inhibiting its power to move freely it won't be 'lithe and active' as the Standard says it should be.

The most important word to remember is 'balance'. That means everything is in harmony together and the proportions right. Make up your mind and stick to it. Don't hover about, the longer you mess about the more likely you are to do the wrong thing, like the bridge player who takes minutes making up his mind what card to play and then invariably chooses the wrong one.

You must get size into your head and you can only do this by acutally measuring your dogs and anyone else's that you can get your hands on. I always remember in my early showing days seeing Dr Tod, a very well-known judge and breeder, go and stand by a dog and look down at her skirt and then I realised she was measuring the height of the dog against herself! Needless to say in those days skirts were worn pretty long. Nowadays one would have to have some mark on one's tights!

Another essential part of being a good judge is the developing of a judging conscience. You will find this will not let you do things that you may want to do but know would be wrong. And always remember, please yourself. People are there wanting your opinion on their dogs. They know their own already and if you judge without fear or favour your opinion will always be respected even if people disagree with you.

Do not judge if it gives you sleepless nights beforehand and you do not enjoy doing it. Always have a reason for what you have done and do not rush into judging before you know what you really want and are looking for.

8　First Aid

There are several good books written by veterinary surgeons about canine diseases and their treatment so I only propose to give a few hints about things that we have found useful in dealing with Shelties. I shall start with what we always keep in our medicine cupboard and why.

A clinical thermometer is the most important thing in the cupboard. At the first sign of a puppy or adult being off colour, take its temperature. 101.1 to 102 degrees is normal. You take it by greasing the end of the thermometer and inserting it about half-an-inch through the anus. Keep hold of the other end — you do not want it disappearing into the lower bowel. If it is a half minute thermometer leave it just over this time. If the temperature is normal there is no need to fuss but if it is over 102 degrees and the dog seems ill call you vet. Other things such as exercise on a hot day may increase the temperature of your dog but he is not ill.

Milk of Magnesia, a bottle of the liquid kind, is the best aperient for dogs. It's also very good to give nursing mothers if they become upset inside after whelping.

You must get a bottle of Streptaquaine Sulpha from your veterinary surgeon. It is wonderful if a puppy or adult has diarrhoea. One teaspoonful twice a day usually puts things right. Continue giving it for at least three days.

Liquid Paraffin is a lubricant and if a dog gets a stoppage it is the safest thing to give. But squeeze a little lemon juice into it to make sure the dog swallows it easily.

Bicarbonate of Soda. If your nursing mother has any trouble with acid milk a large pinch of this on the back of her tongue is a great help; in fact, it is advisable if you know she suffers from this to give her a pinch on the tongue every day for the last week before she whelps and then on for the next ten days. Also, if it is damped, it makes a good dressing to put on a burn or sting.

Talking of burns, the moment the burn has taken place pour cold water over it or put under the cold tap for a minute or two. If this is done at once, it should stop the skin sloughing off.

Soda Mint Tablets. If you have a dog that has rumbling tummy and passes wind, making a nasty smell, two soda mints will put matters right in no time at all.

Savlon disinfectant. We like it best but Dettol or TCP will do. Salvon ointment, the most soothing ointment to put on sores or bites, helps heal and reduces swelling.

Bottle of Benzl Benzoate. A dab of this on a spot or rash has a wonderful effect and on patches of wet eczema it stops irritation and promotes healing.

Kur-Mange is to give your dog a bath in if it has lice or fleas.

White Vaseline can be used to grease your thermometer with. Some people use it to grease the bitches vagina before mating. I prefer to use K-Y lubricating jelly or White Vaseline.

Tes-Tape, from E. Lilly and Co, is useful to see if your bitch is ready for mating. I won't say it is infallible but it does give you a guide. When people bring you a bitch and say, 'I am not sure when she came in,' if the tape shows no green colour you can be sure the bitch is either not ready or is over. It is also useful to find out the bitches who mate at unusual times; say the fifth or sixth day or even the sixteenth or seventeenth. You break a bit of the tape off the roll and insert it up the vagina. Leave it for a few seconds, then remove it. If it shows green or turns green quite quickly, the bitch is ready. If it takes half an hour or so before turning she is not nearly ready. Be sure there is no sugar on your fingers when handling the tape.

Finnons Salts. If you have an old dog who suffers from rheumatism a large pinch on his food every day often helps.

All-Bran, or bran that is given to horses, is useful if you have a dog whose motions are always on the loose side. A small handful put on his meal seems to control it, but you should look to your feeding. There may be something you are giving him that he cannot digest properly; for instance some dogs cannot take milk when they are adult.

Roll of cotton wool.

Scissors, curved, round ended ones for cutting for dew-claws. We use a candle to sterilize them. Hold them in the flame; it makes them hot and so you get the mimimum of bleeding. You can also use them to cut young puppies' toe nails.

Optrex eyedrops to wash the eyes out if a dog gets sawdust, pollen or grass seeds in them. You can also make your own lotion with a solution of bicarbonate, one level teaspoon in half a pint of boiled water but this must be used freshly made.

The following you must get from your veterinary surgeon: *eye ointment, worm pills, flea powder, ear drops.* Shelties on the whole very rarely have ear canker but sometimes old dogs do seem to pick it up and if you have cats they sometimes pass it on, so it is handy to have something you can quickly put in the ear.

Remember that a stich in time saves nine and at the first hint of anything seriously wrong call your veterinary surgeon at once. Prompt action by him may save bad trouble.

The modern dog owners do not realise how lucky they are that the days of distemper epidemics, when whole kennels were wiped out, are over. Now one can have one's puppy immunized against distemper, Hard Pad, Hepatitis and both the *Leptospira — ictevohaemorrhagiae*, which usually causes jaundice, and canicola which is the usual cause of nephritis. The time to have your puppy done is when it is twelve weeks. It will want a second one of the *Leptospira* ten days later. It you have to take a young puppy somewhere where it may come in contact with infection, there is a short term vaccine. It can be given, but the puppy will still want the full immunization at twelve weeks.

Fleas, Ticks, Lice and Harvest Bugs

Fleas are the most common of the parasites that attack dogs. There are various insecticides for dealing with them. It is best to get one from your veterinary surgeon as some of the proprietary ones are harmful to animals as well as fleas.

In the summer when the ground is dry and dusty they can become a menace but we have found a way to keep the kennels clear with the minimum of trouble. For nine years now we have hung a Vapona Strip in each kennel, a large one in the kennels where several dogs are housed and a wardrobe-size one in the single kennels. They are not cheap and want renewing every three months but they are so effective I think it is money well spent. It is such a relief to have dogs that are perfectly clear of parasites and also there are no flies in the kennels. People do say that these strips are harmful but we have had no ill effects in nine years' use and are always on the look out for trouble.

In winter, it is quite a good thing to put a dusting of Cooper's Louse Powder in the bottom of the beds before putting in the bedding. The house dogs pose more of a problem. I was once told by a veterinary surgeon that any wickerwork, such as baskets, dogs beds or arm chairs, are the perfect home for fleas and extremely difficult to disinfect.

We have found a very good balanced mixture of insecticides called Cromocide. One tablespoonful to one pint of water seems to spell instant death to fleas. The makers supply a spray and it is easy to go over the baskets and beds, also any fur rugs where the dogs lie.

Some dogs are allergic to fleas and have only to pick up one to come out in sore places, scratch out handfuls of hair and then the whole skin goes hot and smelly. Luckily it is only the odd dog that is affected in this way but, if kept clear of fleas, is perfectly all right.

You are not likely to find ticks on your dog unless you walk in woods where there is bracken or on moors or fields where there are sheep. Ticks usually attach themselves to some part of the dog's head. You have to take care getting them off to see that the head comes away, otherwise, if it is left in the dog, it may make a nasty sore. Some people say touch them with a lighted cigarette and they will drop off but not being a smoker I take a firm hold, give a twist and jerk them off.

Lice are like tiny ticks. The best way to get rid of them is to bath the dog in Kur-Mange. Your dogs should not have lice. If they do it means the kennels or sheds where they live are dirty and the dogs bedding is wrong. Oat straw for some reason seems to harbour them and should never be used. Wheat straw is best but must be changed pretty frequently.

Harvest bugs or mites are so small they can hardly be seen by the naked eye. They look like orange pollen and usually come between the toes or round the ears where they cause intense irritation. They are very regional and are generally bad on chalk. At our old home, the dogs and cats suffered as well as ourselves but where we are now there do not seem to be any. Flea powder or a dab of surgical spirit between the toes and round the base of the ears should clear them up.

Mange

There are two sorts of mange, sarcoptic and follicula. For some reason you rarely seem to get cases nowadays. I do not know whether it is because animal hygiene has so improved or people take greater care of their dogs and spot it in its early stages.

Sarcoptic, if caught early, is comparatively easy to cure but at one time follicular was considered practically incurable and you were advised to have your dog put down if it had the bad luck to catch it. Thank heavens, this is now a thing of the past.

Follicular can be cured but as in most things the earlier it is diagnosed the better, so if your dog develops a small bare patch on its face, this is where follicular usually starts, get a scraping done by your veterinary surgeon as soon as possible and if it is follicular and he says it is incurable go to someone else.

Or it may be ringworm. If you live on a farm and the dogs come in contact with cattle they may easily pick it up and so may you! I know as I have caught it from cattle. In the end my doctor gave me up and sent me to my veterinary surgeon who cured me with one application of an ointment used on calves.

Eclampsia

This affects nursing bitches, usually ones that are extra good mothers and drain all their calcium away for the puppies. It is much the same thing as milk fever in cows. The remedy is to get your veterinary surgeon at once to give the bitch an injection of calcium. The bitch may just collapse and go into a coma or she may start off by looking drunk and staggering about. Once she's had the calcium injection she should recover pretty quickly but it is wisest to take her away from her puppies. It usually comes on when the pups are three or four weeks as that is when they are being the biggest drain on their dam.

If a bitch has eclampsia once it does not mean she will always have it, because you can be extra careful and see she gets plenty of calcium and Vitamin D all the time she is feeding her puppies.

Heat Stroke

This is very alarming. The dog staggers about and then collapses and lies gasping on the ground, eyes popping. Quickly lay him out in the shade where the air is moving, pour cold water down his spine, get ice cubes from the fridge, put them in a polythene bag and hold them on his head. Get in touch with your vet and he will give a heart stimulant if he thinks it necessary. The dog must be kept very quiet for several days.

You see dogs at shows when the weather is hot collapsing and sometimes dying from heat stroke. Bulldogs are particularly susceptible. Never leave a dog in a car in hot weather, even with the windows open it soon becomes like an oven and a dog will collapse very soon in these conditions. People are extremely stupid over this as everybody must have got into a car that's been standing in the sun and been unable to touch the seats with a bare hand. Just think what it must be like to be shut in and not be able to get out.

Car Sickness

Unfortunately Shelties seem very prone to this but they do usually seem to grow out of it in time. There are several things one can try with a puppy. Leave it in a stationary car and feed it there so it gets used to the smell and associates it with food. Take it for very short journeys to start with, only a few minutes in the car, and then somewhere nice where it can have a gallop or play about so it connects going in a car with fun.

You can help things by giving the pup some of the seasick remedies that are made for children and Shaw's Travel Sickness pills work well with most dogs. You want to experiment with different ones till you find one that suits your pup and after it has done a journey or two without being sick you will find that it no longer needs a pill. I know it is very exasperating and sometimes I have wished I had a breed that got straight into a car and was never sick from the word go.

9 Male Lines

CHE Male Lines

Until 1939 the CHE male line produced the most C.C. winners and was much the strongest. It still is in the United States. It started with a dog called Nesting Topper who sired Ashbank Olla. This dog not only sired Irvine Ronnie, Chestnut Rainbow's sire, but Tit Bit who went on to produce the four famous Eltham Park champions, Elda, Elfine, Evan and Evette. There, unfortunately, that male line died out, whereas Chestnut Rainbow, who incidentally gives his name to the Line, not only sired fived dogs who bred on, but two outstanding bitches: Ch. Redbraes Magda and Ch. Tilford Tontine, the dam of four champions. (Only two others have done that to date — Ch's. Riverhill Rare Gold and Riverhill Rather Rich).

Nut of Houghton Hill was the most important of the dogs as he sired Ch. Uam Var of Houghton Hill, the line that is going strong today. All these dogs were tricolours. Redbraes Rollo was the other important son. He was responsible for Ch. Gawaine of Camelaird so was behind Arthur of Camelaird and Peabody Paul.

Ch. Uam Var sired three champions and three C.C. winners. His champion daughter, Blue Blossom of Houghton Hill, was one of the most important brood bitches but it is through his sons Yes Tor of Houghton Hill and Golden Spider of Houghton Hill that the CHE line goes on today.

Yes Tor sired Beacon of Houghton Hill just at the end of the last war. Beacon was the most elegant, sound dog and very showy. Mrs. Baker was getting old and couldn't get him to shows but he was a lovely dog. He sired Honour Bright of Surreyhills, the first Ob. Ch. bitch and also Ch. Bonfire of Exford, one of the first post war champions and a little beauty. Through his son Houghton Hill Sniper, a small tricolour — almost a black and tan — he went down to Surprise Packet of Exford, a blue merle who, incidentally, was a monorchid, and who sired two champions and two C.C. winners, one of whom, Cracker of Exford, sired Ch. Pop Gun of Exford. This line is now represented by Ch. Drumcauchlie Bumble Boy who has sired Ch. Salroyds Buzzer among his first crop.

Golden Spider sired Ch. Moneyspinner of Exford; Ch. Mazurka of Houghton Hill, another very important bitch; Spinning Coin of Exford, who was responsible for, among others, Ch. Spendthrift of Exford, Fetlar Jackanapes, the sire of Ch. Fetlar Magnus and the only dog between the wars twice to be Best of Breed at the E.S.S.C. Show.

Ch. Moneyspinner of Exford's most important son was Ch. Riverhill Rufus. Most of the present day CHE's come through his two sons, Philabeg of Crawleyridge and Rufus of Edingley. Philabeg comes down to Ch. Exford Piskiegye Taw through his son Ch. Lothario of Exford and grandson Ch. Philander of Exford to Ch. Bystars Wee Laddie.

Through Rufus of Edingley come the two litter brothers Ch. Delwood Terence and Ellington Encore. Terence is the grandsire of Ch. Viking of Melvaig whose son Ch. Wattawoodcut is responsible for Ch. Greenscrees Swordsman and his crop of champions and C.C. winners. Viking's other well known son was Ch. Dilhorne Norseman of Melvaig, sire of Ch. Dilhorne Blackcap who in turn sired eight champions. Ellington Encore was the early leading post-war sire as he had six champions and five C.C. winners to his credit. Unfortunately, the male line here seems to more or less come to a dead end as nearly all his champions were bitches.

Ch. Dilhorne Norseman of Melvaig, a Viking of Melvaig son.

A famous sire: Ch.
Riverhill Rufus
(1935).

Ch. Riverhill Rufus had the most enormous effect on the breed and
although he sired only one champion himself, he was a wonderful sire
of brood bitches and he is behind every Riverhill pedigree.

Ch. Viking of Melvaig
(1951), a famous CHE
sire.

I should like to make some personal remarks about the most important
old dogs as soon there will not be anyone who has seen them in the flesh.

In this line Ch. Uam Var of Houghton Hill was a small, sturdy tricolour with a wonderful one-piece head and a very good eye; he was
heavy-coated which made him appear rather low to the ground. Yes Tor
of Houghton Hill was a small tricolour with very rich red tan and good
coat but did not have the head of Uam Var. Golden Spider of Houghton
Hill was sable but never seen and reputed to have Collie blood very close
up; in fact someone who did see him said he looked like a Collie on
short legs. His son Ch. Moneyspinner of Exford was a wonderful headed
dog, shaded sable with not much coat and what he had was curly, and
very intelligent. He went everywhere with his mistress, even into cinemas.
His son, Ch. Riverhill Rufus was smaller, a rich red gold and bred true
for sable. His head was a model with the sweetest expression; again not
much coat and his shoulder could have been better. He had the most
gentle nature but was always top dog in the kennel; he only had to look
at a dog to quell a riot.

His son, Philabeg of Crawleyridge, was shaded sable, small but not
the head of his father and with a curly tail. He was rather a second string
as his owner Col. Russell had had a lovely dog by Rufus whom he thought

Ch. Wattawoodcut (1957) son of Viking of Melvaig.

was the best he had ever bred, but it died of distemper; in desperation he sent another bitch to Rufus just as the war started and the result was Philabeg. But although he had not the looks of his father or half-brother he did prove a good sire and his great-grandson, Ch. Exford Piskiegye Taw was a golden sable, lovely size and a real racing machine. One of his charms for me was that he always smelt strongly of Harris Tweed. He was the exception to prove the rule that Shelties do not hunt as he was run over and killed while hunting in the New Forest, but luckily had left some good ones behind him: Ch. Crag of Exford, who went to the U.S.A. and did well there, and, incidentally, was the only dog ever to beat Ch. Helensdale Ace; and Ch. Lothario of Exford. Both these dogs were tricolours, Lothario was a real galloping dog like his sire, but heavier built. He sired champions of all three colours. His most modern representative is his grandson Ch. Bystars Wee Laddie who has a great look of Ch. Uam Var of Houghton Hill.

Rufus of Edingley was never seen by the general public but I was told by someone that they had used him because he had a head like our Ch. Riverhill Rufus. I fancy there was Collie blood somewhere around as I remember his dam when she came to be mated was large and very Collie-like. Anyhow his son Ellington Eddy sired Ch. Delwood Terence who

Ch. Riverhill Rogue (1958), the only post-war Sheltie to have won two C.C.s at Crufts.

was a golden sable, on the big side, with a strong foreface and good eye. His son Delwood Bobby was a small dark red sable with hardly any white. He sired Ch. Viking of Melvaig, also a rich dark sable, small and with a lovely quality one-piece head and very good eye. His hocks were his failing.

His son, Ch. Wattawoodcut, was a golden sable with a lot of white on his face. He was larger than his sire and sturdy, but he hadn't his father's quality head and eye, whereas his son Ch. Greenscrees Swordsman, a golden sable, had. He sired five champions and five C.C. winners, and is going on through his son Ch. Greenscrees Nobleman, who has two present day champion sons in Ch. Forestland Briar and Ch. Snabswood Summer Wine of Willowtarn; and another son Ch. Prunepark's Jason Junior has also sired a recent champion in Garlea Iona Lad, so there is no chance of this line dying out at present. Ch. Viking's other son Ch. Dilhorne Norseman of Melvaig was a real example of the 'lithe and graceful' dog called for by the Standard. I shall never forget seeing him come into the ring at Crufts; it was his first show, how much more interesting it was in the

Another famous sire,
Ch. Dilhorne Blackcap
(1956).

days before dogs had to qualify and a new face could come into the ring and sweep the board. I thought when I handled him, 'There is my probable Best of Breed' – and so it turned out. He was a tricolour, 14½ inches, fit to run for his life. He worked a large flock of sheep and belonged to a farmer. He had a lovely balance all through with good bone and that 'look of eagles' so lacking in most dogs. He went on to get his title that year at the E.S.S.C. championship show where he was Best in Show.

Although only at stud for a short time – his owner got fed up with stud work – he sired Ch. Dilhorne Blackcap, Ch. Pied Piper of Melvaig and Riverhill Reckless, sire of Ch. Riverhill Rogue who followed his grandsire by going Best of Breed at Crufts and Best in Show at the E.S.S.C. championship show in the same year.

Ch. Dilhorne Blackcap was twice Best in Show at the E.S.S.C. championship show and proved a top sire with eight champions to his credit. He was a tricolour, a good deal larger and stronger than his sire but with a lovely smooth one-piece head. Unfortunately one of his champion sons was run over and killed; one went to the States and the third was a blue merle and they have a limited stud use, but his champion daughters have made a name for themselves.

Ch. Delwood Terence's litter brother, Ellington Encore, was a red gold sable, just too big to show. He again had a lovely one-piece head and was a most effective sire with six champions and five C.C. winners. Again, he had only one champion son, Ellington Esquire, who went out to America before he had been used very much, but he did sire Ch. Cutie of Knockmahar, a really top class sable bitch. He also sired Fielder of Foula who was the sire of Ch. Lovelight of Lydwell, one of the top class show and brood bitches, but the male line has not gone on – by that I mean by not producing C.C. winners. But who knows, they may turn up again at any time as there must be some of his blood about still in other dogs.

When I say a Line or Family has not bred on or died out, there is always a chance it will turn up C.C. winners again several generations later. This happens more often in the bitch families. I had to take one recent champion back thirteen generations before it linked up with a known member of a C.C. winning family, whereas in the male line five generations seems to have been the limit.

BB Male Line

Since the 1950s and BBs have forged ahead and now outnumber the CHEs. The line started with Butcher Boy. That he was sable is known but nothing more; his son Wallace was sable too. There is a photograph of him; he looks to have heavy ears and rather a Terrier-like head. He sired two important dogs, both sables, in Rip of Mountfort, who had several champions and C.C. winners descended from him but no male line going on at present; and War Baby of Mountfort, who through his son Rufus of Mountfort, a C.C. winner, and Rufus's son Ch. Specks of Mountfort (who in turn sired Ch. Eltham Park Eureka) is responsible for all the present day BB's.

Eureka was a very heavy-coated sable with, I was told, a rather short tail. I never actually saw him but in his photograph he looks very Collie-like. He sired Max of Clerwood, a tricolour whose great grandson was Ch. Kinnersley Gold Dust, bred by Mrs Kinnersley Taylor who sold him to Mr Tom Care who showed him and made him up. Mr Care then passed him on to the Hon. Mrs Berry, now Mrs Seys. I took a great interest in this dog as at my first judging appointment he was my Best of Breed. He was a lovely rich red gold sable with a full white collar, a very nice size and balanced all through; a dog that could win today.

He is important as he sired Fydell Startler, a dreary tricolour, small and stocky with a lovely head rather like Ch. Uam Var of Houghton Hill. He was being shown before the last war and then won a C.C. after the war was over which was good going and showed his lasting qualities. He sired Ch. Helensdale Bhan so is behind all the string of Helensdale champions. He also sired Ch. Fydell Round Up. Funnily enough, I gave both these dogs C.C.s. Bhan was a mahogany sable, a small dog and very attractive to look at but not a good mover.

Round Up was a shaded sable, very nice head and good eye, rather long in the back and a difficult dog to show. Poor Mr Broughton, his owner, went through agonies trying to get him to show his ears. At one time it looked as if he would never get his title, but he made it in the end and sired three champions and a C.C. winner, but none are going on in the male line though his champion daughter Riverhill Rugosa is the main stay of Family 24.

Returning to Ch. Helensdale Bhan, he sired three champions and five C.C. winners. By far his best son was Ch. Helensdale Ace. Bhan got out by mistake and mated his dam Helensdale Gentle Lady and the result was Ace!

Whereas Fydell Startler was a very dreary tricolour with little or no white, his son Bhan was a dark mahogany with some white, but not all that glamorous. Ace was glamour personified, in spite of his crooked white blaze. He was the colour of his dam's sire, Ch. Nicky of Abelour, more of whom comes later. You could pick Ace to pieces as he was full of faults, but he'd still come back at you and knock you for six. His personality and glamour were terrific, you couldn't see anything else while he was in the ring. At his first show, when he was only just six months, he won the puppy class. His sire won open but it was Ace who got the C.C. and his dad had to be content with the Res. C.C.

It wasn't surprising he was such an outstanding sire; he had such character. He was a fiery red with a good deal of white. He passed his colour and markings, including his crooked blaze, on to his sons and daughters which included more C.C. winners than any other dog has sired to date — ten champions and ten C.C. winners. His son Ch. Alasdair of Tintobank beat him by one in champions — eleven — but only had four C.C. winners.

Bhan had another son that did very well at stud in Helensdale Frolic. He was on the big side but had a really nice head and personality. He sired five champions and three C.C. winners. He goes on today through his son Ch. Sumburgh Sirius and grandsons Ch. Sumburgh Little Hercules and Ch. Tyneford Tarsus.

Another Bhan grandson to do well was Ch. Francis of Merrion. He was a small, stocky golden sable and at one time held the record for C.C.s won. He sired two champions, one being Ch. Cheluth Twinkleberry, and is behind one other and three C.C. winners, all bitches.

Six of Ace's champions were bitches. His first one, Riverhill Royal Flush, was one of the foundation bitches of the Shelerts. Helensdale

Ch. Skye of Whytelaw, winner of his sixth C.C. at the age of nine.

Wendy and Waxwing both went abroad. Helensdale Lena and Crochmaid Sunstar did not breed on, but Shady Fern of Sheldawyn has a great grandson champion, Anchor of Sheldawyn.

Ace's son Ch. Laird of Whytelaw has left his mark. His grandson Ch. Skye of Whytelaw was an outstanding dog; a lovely rich red who stood foursquare, who won a sixth C.C. at the age of nine. Two other grandsons, Ch. Sweetsultan of Shelert who although he sired four champion sons and three others who sired champions, all seemed to run to bitches; the other grandson, Ch. Luna Andy of Upperslaughter, is grandsire to Ch. Exford Pipestyle Mystic Star, a dual C.C. winner at the E.S.S.C. championship show and Happy Man of Exford, a C.C. winner.

Ch. Alasdair of Tintobank, the most famous of Ace's sons, was a rather dull shaded sable. His dam was a tricolour and he usually sired at least one tricolour in a litter. But in spite of his rather dreary appearance he had great presence and, as I have said before, sired eleven champions. Unfortunately he had double jointed hocks and could on occasions stand like a Chow. In some degree he passed this on. His first champion, Riverhill Rare Gold, had them but not nearly so pronounced and she did not pass them on. Besides Rare Gold he sired some lovely bitches — Ch.s Diadem of Callart, Honeybunch of Melvaig, Brigdale Romaris, Crochmaid Starlight, Love Sonnett of Lydwell, Beathag of Tintobank; and the dogs Ch.s Struan of Callart, Kendoral Ulysses, Trumpeter of Tonneytown and Ireland's Eye Trefoil of Arolla, who did so much for the Irish Shelties.

Mr Guthrie's luck was certainly in when he bought Alasdair's dam in whelp from Mr Saunders when she was carrying him. Funnily enough, Alasdair's line at one moment hung by a thread when Ch. Riverhill Rampion went to Australia where he became top sire for several years and has sired thirty-five champions; another of Alasdair's sons, Ch. Honeyboy of Callart, went to Canada. Now the line goes on through Mantoga Zircon of Kabul, a C.C. winner and Ch. Trumpeter of Tooneytown, whose latest descendants are Ch. Loughrigg Kings Minstrel who has already sired a champion bitch and Ch. Midnitesun Justin Time a Group winner. Ch. Hallinwood Flash, another Ace son, sired two champions and four C.C. winners, but has no active dog line. On the other hand, Ch. Hazelhead Gay Wanderer, another Ace son, is going on in direct line through his son Ch. Penvose Brandy Snap, Ch. Riverhill Ratafia, Ch. Rodhill Burnt Sugar, Ch. Riverhill Ricotta, Ch. Haytimer of Hanburyhill at Hartmere, and also through Ricotta's brother Riverhill Roux, sire of Ch. Mistmere Marking Time at Stornaway and the C.C. winner Riverhill Roquefort. Another line from Penvose Brandy Snap goes down to English and Irish champion Cregagh Student Prince at stud in Eire. So there is no danger of Ace's line dying out at present, although he was a monorchid. In fact a great many champions in this period were monorchids. Dogs born in and around 1948 to 1952 seemed to suffer this way. I often wondered if it was because their parents had been born during the war or just after, and whether feeding had anything to do with it.

Besides Ace there were Ch. Orpheus of Callart, Ch. Exford Piskiegye Taw, Ch. Viking of Melvaig, Ch. Riverhill Rikki and Ch. Francis of Merrion, besides various C.C. winners and other dogs that were used quite a bit. It is not a common fault in the present day Sheltie, so one wonders if it is so very hereditary. After all, if it were, with the amount of Ace, Taw, Orpheus and Viking blood in the present day Sheltie, one would not expect there to be an entire dog in the breed today.

Eureka's other son was Eltham Park Evolution, whose dam was a Collie. He sired Blinx of Clerwood, a tricolour with one bright blue eye. In spite of this he won a C.C. and sired Ch. Euan of Clerwood, a rich mahogany, on the large side and with rather light eyes. He sired a champion and three C.C. winners, all Clerwoods, none of them going on. Harvey was Blinx's most important son. He was sable and lived in the North; I never saw him but he is the great-grandfather of Ch. Nicky of Abelour.

Ch. Nicky of Aberlour, a famous BB sire.

If I could pick only one dog from the BB line I would settle for Nicky. Unfortunately there is not a photograph that does him justice. He was quite outstanding. I gave him his third C.C. at Crufts 1939. He had a really wonderful coat, fiery red gold with a full white collar, rather a wide white blaze, but evenly marked, very good eye and perfect ears. He, too, had the look of eagles. His conformation was much better than that of his grandson Ace. Ace, too, had that presence that denotes a great dog. I gave him a C.C. as well, but if the two had met it would have been Nicky first.

Of course, the war put a brake on what Nicky could have done for the breed. Thank heavens, though, Mr Hendry did not send him out to the States at the start of the war, although he had a tempting offer for him. He told me he loved seeing Nicky around the place and decided to keep him at home. I hate to think what the breed would have missed if he had gone. I saw Nicky again after the war. His head was better than when he was being shown, but he had had hard pad badly and it had left his hind legs rather crippled. But it still gave one pleasure to look at him.

Of course the war was a tragedy where he was concerned as he was hardly used at all. He lived so far North in Scotland that apart from ourselves I think the only southern breeders who used him were Mrs Charlton

Ch. Riverhill Redcoat, a son of Nicky of Aberlour.

whose Ch. Viking of Melvaig had two lines to him; Miss Gwynne-Jones's great brood bitch Heatherbell of Callart (the dam of two champions and a C.C. winner) was by him.

In Scotland, Mr J. Saunders had Ace's dam, Helensdale Gentle Lady, and we had Ch. Riverhill Redcoat, a shaded sable, beautifully sound and with a regal head carriage and perfect eye. But he had desperately prick ears so he could never go in more than one class as I couldn't keep them over for longer. Both his parents had beautiful natural ears — so much for hereditary — and he did not sire a lot of prick-eared puppies. It must have just been a personal idiosyncrasy. He sired five champions. His son Ch. Russetcoat of Callart, a shaded sable like his sire, sired Ch. Heatherisle Rufus, a beautiful headed dog called Rufus by his breeder Mrs Hawkins as she said he reminded her of Riverhill Rufus. He is going on through Ch. Skirl of Shelert.

Redcoat's son, Ensign of Oastwood, sired Ch. Brigdale Renown, a small sable dog who before he went to Canada sired Ch. Midas of Shelert, who was the most spectacular dog, a rich red gold who really looked like galloping. Unfortunately, he loathed shows, but was the sort of dog who could have won groups if he had put it all in. He sired three champions and is going on via his grandson Ch. Sea Urchin of Shelert, a pale gold who never carried much coat but was a very racy looking dog; and Sea Urchin's grandsons Ch. Strict Tempo of Shelert, Ch. Winston of Joywil and Ch. Riverhill Richman. Richman is going on through his son Ch. Riverhill Ringmaster, grandson Riverhill Ringsider and great grandson Ch. Nitelife Rogue Star and another son Ch. Brigdale Play Boy. Strict Tempo of Shelert goes on through his grandson Ch. Felthorn Beachcomber and his son Ch. Franchill Beach Boy.

The other important Aberlour dog was Harvey's great-great-grandson Hector of Abelour. Not a patch on Nicky to look at, he was never shown as he was too big, but I did see him. He was a shaded sable, heavy coated with a very Collie-type head with small prick ears that were torn with fighting. It is unusual for a Sheltie to be a fighter, but he did not seem to pass it on as neither his son Ch. Orpheus of Callart, a very taking golden sable for whom I always had a soft spot as I handled him to win two of his C.C.s as he would not co-operate with his owner in the ring — nor Orpheus's son Ch. Riverhill Rescuer, a rich-shaded sable who was the gentlest dog and never showed any pugnacious tendancies.

Rescuer's grandson, Ch. Ebony Pride of Glenhill, was a really beautiful tricolour. He sailed through to win nine C.C.s, then he was tragically run over when being exercised by a child. This is a fate that has struck down so many well-known Shelties and always seems such a pitiful waste. He sired Ch. Golden Thread of Exford and two C.C. winners but he goes on through his son Carousel of Melvaig who was out of a very good bitch, Ch. Honeybunch of Melvaig. He never did much winning but was

Ch. Sharval the
Deliquent (1969),
record holder of fif-
teen C.C.s.

a well made sable, rather thick in skull and had rather low carried ears.
He was a very good sire and got three champions and three C.C. winners.

One of his champions is Sharval the Delinquent, a very dark tricolour
who holds the present record for C.C.s won, fifteen in all. The Delinquent
is going on through his son, Ch. Rhinog The Gay Lancer, who has sired
a champion, and another son, Ch. Sandpiper of Sharval, who has earned
the distinction of being the first Sheltie to win a Best in Show at a
championship show, Belfast, also two Working Groups. Both these sons
are sables.

One of Carousel's C.C. winners, Riverhill Rolling Home, was the first
Sheltie dog to sire Group Winners; Ch. Antoc Sealodge Spotlight won the
Non-Sporting Group at Bournemouth before it was split into Working
and Utility; Ch. Deloraine Dilys of Monkswood won the Working Group
at Cruft's. Another Rolling Home son, Strikin' Midnight at Shelert,
has sired nine champions, eight of them dogs, of which seven
have sired C.C. winners. One, Ch. Such a Spree at Shelert, a beautiful

coloured blue merle who himself has sired two Ch. blue merle dogs, Such a Frolic and Such a Gamble both at Shelert; the first named has a champion daughter. Frolic's little sister, Ch. She's my Fancy at Shelert, I consider one cf the best Sheltie bitches there has been and certainly the best blue merle; she is a Working Group winner. Such a Spree's litter brother, Ch. Such a Beano at Shelert, a tricolour, has a sable grandson Ch. Fairona Rockafella based in Scotland. Another Strikin' Midnight son, Ch. Dilhorne Jester, a tricolour, sired Ch. Dilhorne Bluemirth, the top winning C.C. bitch and English and Irish Ch. Cregagh Tarfin Blue Melody. Ch. Special Edition of Shelert, another Strikin' Midnight sable son, goes on through his son Ch. Sail Ho at Shelert. Another champion son of Strikin' Midnight was the tricolour Ch. Hildlane Ministrel Knight who, in turn, sired Ch. Hildlane Winters Night, also a tricolour and very like his sire. Hildlane Minstrel Knight is also the grandsire of Ch. Lirren Evening Shadow at Ramtin, a small almost black and tan dog.

Ch. Antoc Sealodge Spotlight, a sable Rolling Home son, was a bright sable and the most wonderful showman with the merriest expression, the sort of dog that made a great many friends for the breed. He had one Ch. son, Loughrigg Dragon Fly, a beautifully headed tricolour who in turn sired Ch. Selskars Cloudberry of Greensands, a good coloured merle who sired a champion bitch before he left for Australia. Dragon Fly was also the grandsire of Ch. Kyleburn Golden Eagle, a showy rich-coloured sable who has sired some lovely champion bitches and has a champion grandson in Ch. Foxlark Fandango, who bares a strong resemblance to him.

Spotlight also sired Glenmist Golden Falcon who in turn sired Ch. Jefsfire Freelancer, a well-marked golden sable, a most successful sire. He had eight champions, five of them dogs, Ch.s Sumburgh Tesoro Zhivago, Scarabrae Sinjon, Scarabrae Statesman, Francehill Persimon and Shelderon Gay Ghillie, as well as C.C. winners. He is also the grand-sire of Ch. Lythwood Brandy Snap and Ch. Cowellekot Crown Prince of Stormane. He also sired Ferdinando of Myriehewe, a C.C. winner who is making a name for himself as a sire — he already has two champion daughters. Glenmist Golden Falcon also sired Ch. Glenmist Gaylord of Jaylea and the C.C. winner Tyneford Token Gold. The sad thing about Golden Falcon was he went blind with P.R.A. This is a point to remember if tempted to inbreed too close to Freelancer.

To go back to Carousel of Melvaig, he is also going on through another son, Tornado of Melvaig who is going on through Ch. Janetstown Jour-nalist and his C.C. winning son Janetstown Jacobean.

There is another line coming down from Ch. Riverhill Rescuer through his son Riverhill Ranger, who sired Ch. Riverhill Raider, a 14-inch pale golden sable, who in turn sired Ch. Monkswood Moss Trooper and Ch. Rhinog Hunky Dory. Hunky Dory sired Ch. Rhinog The Black Watch,

Ch. Jefsfire Freelancer,
a great sire.

a Crufts C.C. winner as was Moss Trooper who in turn sired Ch. Mistmere Marching Orders, also a Crufts C.C. winner and who is responsible
for the 1979 Crufts winner Ch. Lythwood Snaffles. Riverhill Ranger's
other champion son Swagman from Shiel, a rich-shaded sable with the
endearing trick of smiling and showing all his teeth in a broad grin, he
sired Ch. Riverhill Rapparee who went to Sweden but goes on through
his son Ch. Durnovaria Double Agent, another Crufts C.C. winner. So
Hector's line is in a very strong position with all these active dogs stemming from him.

CHE and BB are the two main Lines. There were five more that sired
C.C. winners, LJA, TPR, IH, LWW and DL, but there are no modern
dogs carrying on from any of these.

There is something else I should like to put on record. In the BB Line,
four generations from Wallace, there is a dog listed as Mountlethen Blue
Prince, who in fact was a blue merle Collie. As I have said elsewhere,
blue merle is a colour unknown in the original Shelties in the Islands, so
this was one of the ways it got into the Sheltie. As he does not go on in
tail male, it was thought better to leave him in the Charts where he was
placed under a misapprehension rather than start another line.

10 Female Families

Female Families

Having written something about the dogs in the CHE and BB Lines, I should like to mention some of the outstanding bitches in the breed who have had a profound effect on the present day Sheltie.

Family 1

I shall start with Family 1. All the early bitches here were Eltham Parks and a great many of the best went to the United States. The key bitches that remained in this country were Ch. Eltham Park Eunice and Eltham Park Estelle; the latter is going strongest today through Helensdale Mhairi Dhu and Helensdale Nighean Dhu and a half-sister Lethellen Sable Queen. Mhairi Dhu and Nighean Dhu were both tricolours as their names tell one, Dhu meaning black. This was rather odd as Helensdales were predominantly sable. Mhairi Dhu was the dam of Ch. Alasdair of Tintobank and the colour factor must have been very strong in Alasdair since, although sable, he nearly always sired at least one tricolour in each litter. The latest winners from this branch of the Family are Ch.'s Heathlow Ermintrude, Mirabell of Monkreddan (now in Australia) Gold Charm of Monkreddan, Monkreddan Sunray and Lathmere Zoe with two C.C.s and her daughter Ch. Jefsfire Rich Reward. Ch. Heathlow Lucianna, besides being a most attractive bitch in her own right, was also the dam of Ch. Jefsfire Freelancer who has sired so many winners.

There are two blue merle champion bitches also coming down through Mhairi Dhu; Ch. Roaming of Exford and Ch. Blue Opal of Heathlow. Helensdale Nighean Dhu has several champion bitches coming down from her but none very active at the moment – Ch. Francehill Light Fantastic, Ch. Gorjess Waltz of Melcette, Ch. Sheer Sauce from Shiel and Ch. Daisy of Whytelaw being some of them. Lethellen Sable Queen, the other half-sister of the two Dhu's comes down eleven generations before producing a champion in Ch. Shelverne Spun Gold.

The part of the Family stemming from Ch. Eltham Park Eunice includes Ch. Eltham Park Elda, a golden sable that ran up a series of C.C. wins before the war. She was a lovely bitch with great charm and presence – one of the greats. She had a C.C. winning son, Delwood

Bubbles, but no line goes on in female descent. There were several well-known champion bitches, Ch.'s Ellington Easter Lady, Ellington Wattlingate Waitress, Rhapsody of Rivoch, Martine of Melvaig, Deirdre Dhu of Glenawind, the black and white Irish champion who had two C.C.s and Rinth Alice of Badgersett who was a Crufts C.C. winner, but so far none of them are going on in the female line. There are several Ob. C.C. winners in the Family, Ch. Rory of Lerwick and Golden Gregory and Rainelor Raven.

Family 2

Family 2 had a lot of C.C. winners in the early twenties, but none of them bred on. The Family goes down today through Ashbank Jean to Lady of Camelaird, a rather large tricolour, a wonderful bright colour with really red tan. She never had a great deal of coat but her daughter Fetlar Vaila, a sable C.C. winner, is the ancestress of the Hartfields and includes Ch. Hartfield Harbinger and the C.C. winners Hartfield Honey and Hartfield High Hopes.

Another of Lady of Camelaird's daughters, Lady of Houghton Hill, has a great many Exford champions and C.C. winners stemming from her. The most important is Ch. Butterfly of Exford, a charming sable, perfect size and as sound as a bell. She bred two champions and two C.C. winners. Ch. Black Moth of Exford was a tricolour edition of her mother. She is behind Ch. Golden Thread of Exford and Ch. Philander of Exford besides several C.C. winners. Black Moth's litter sister Ch. Honeysuckle of Exford was sable but to my mind not so attractive as her sister. She was the dam of Ch. Pop Gun of Exford and Honeydew of Exford, a C.C. winner.

Another of Butterfly's descendants was Ch. Melody of Exford, a tricolour. She in turn had a grand-daughter Ch. Sharval Burlesque, a blue merle; and another, Sharval Cilla Black, the dam of three champions, Sharval Merle Oberon, Sharval The Delinquent and Sharval Small Dark 'n' Handsome, now in Holland.

Yet another line from Lady of Houghton Hill produced Ch. Heatherisle Rufus and Lucy Locket from Ifieldwood, a duel C.C. winner.

Going back to Ashbank Jean, she was great-grandmother of Ch. Rob Roy O'Pages Hill who started life as a Helensdale but had his name changed when he was bought by Mr W. Gallagher. He was campaigned in this country, won his title and then went to the States where he soon became an American champion and a pillar of the breed.

Family 3

Family 3 is the Chestnut family, Chestnut Sweet Lady being the key bitch. She was a tricolour, rather dipped in the back. Her daughter Ch. Redbraes Madga was a very attractive tricolour owned by Dr Margaret Todd of the Clerwoods. She comes down through Peabody Peggy, a small showily marked tricolour. She was the dam of Ch. Peabody Peggoty and Peabody Pegantree who is behind two lovely bitches, Ch. Runlee Phantasy and Ch. Wravella of Wyndora. Sadly enough neither are going on at present.

The line that all the present day Family 3 comes from, bar one, is a third daughter of Peggy, Jill of Mariemeau, who in turn was dam of Mariemeau Black Bonnet. It is worth putting on record that this bitch was white with a tricolour head and a black patch on her body.

I think my sister and I were two of the very few people ever to penetrate Mrs James's walled orchard and so see this bitch and her daughter Rona of Pemellan, who was marked like a skewbald horse. She proved a very important bitch with two champion grand-daughters — Ellington Enjoyment, the first post-war champion bitch; and Ch. Ardene Asta, who was great-grandmother of Ch. Lovelight of Lydwell. Lovelight was not only a very good show bitch but also a splendid brood bitch. She had two champion daughters and three C.C. winners and a daughter,

Ch. Sandpiper of Sharval (1978) winner of two Working Groups and Best in Show.

Quendale Love Ballade of Lydwell from whom Ch. Delamere Lady Miss Cherie is descended. From her champion daughter Love's Serendade of Lydwell, are descended Ch; Cheluth Blackberry, a very charming well made tricolour that was a Crufts winner and Ch. Heathlow Priscilla and also the C.C. winner Wellswood Charming Cherry who has an Ob. C.C. winning daughter, Rodhill Frosted Cherry. Lovelight's C.C. winning daughter Latest Love of Lydwell is behind Ch. Penvose Cherry Brandy and the C.C. winners Jaysgarth Sable Silk of Fairlow and Trethosa Artful Lass.

From Dainty Lady, another Black Bonnet daughter, Ch. Day Dawning of Tynereoch stems. A third daughter, Mariemeau Katrine, has the most modern C.C. winners — several champion dogs in Rhinog the Black Watch, Rodhill Burnt Sugar, Selskars Cloudberry of Greensands, now in Australia as is the C.C. winner Ellendale Etienne. Further back come three Fydell C.C. winning dogs. The bitches are Ch. Trennaway Electa and Ch. Wellswood Amberrae, several C.C. winners, both dogs and bitches, and the latest champion Skerrywood Sandstorm. The only other modern C.C. bitch winner in Family 3 that doesn't come down through Ch. Redbraes Magda is Deborah of Cragside, who stems from the C.C. winner Wendy of Wyndora, also coming from Wendy of Wyndora is Ch. Sandpiper of Sharval, the first Sheltie to win a Best in Show at a general championship show, Belfast 1978.

Family 4

Ch. Tilford Tontine dominates this family. She had two champion sons, Tilford Tay and Tweed, and two champion daughters, Tinette who went to the States, and Ch. Mary of Camevock owned in partnership by Miss Thynne and Miss Allen, hence the joint affix made of half their affixes, Camelaird and Kilravock. Tontine was a lovely bitch, tricolour, very advanced in head for her time. She didn't carry very much coat. Her daughter Mary was a sable, and a real quality bitch. I knew her well as she was lent to us in 1939 to breed a litter while Mrs Allen was in hospital. We mated her to Ch. Spendthrift of Exford. The litter was a few weeks old when war was declared. It was a difficult time and we gave the puppies away. One went to Mrs Sangster and became Extravagance of Exford, grand-dam of Ch. Bonfire of Exford, one of the early post war champions. We kept what we thought was the best one and put her out on breeding terms, but when we came to suggest she had a litter her owners had vanished complete with dog, so a really good bitch was lost to the breed. Bonfire was a lovely little tricolour, all quality. She had Ch. Firebrand of Exford whose descendants include Ch. Moonshadow of Sheldawyn and Ch's Debonair of Exford and Rockaround Blue Gamble.

The line from another Tontine daughter, Tilford Titania, produced the Ch.'s Una Jane and Dileas of the Wansdyke, the latter the most lovely sound mover, a joy to look at; it also produced Ch. Bystars Wee Laddie.

Family 5

This is Ch. Nicky of Aberlour's family. The odd thing is that out of forty-five C.C. winners only thirteen are bitches, so it is a family that produces good dogs. The line that is going strong is through Riverhill Reinette and her daughters Ch. Riverhill Regale and Reina. They are responsible for all the present day Family 5 winners. Reinette was a golden sable, a real charmer, born during the war and from the last litter sired by Ch. Riverhill Rufus. Her daughter Ch. Riverhill Regale bred Ch. Riverhill Royal Flush, bought as a puppy by the Misses Herbert as one of their foundation bitches. She was the dam of their first home bred champion Midas of Shelert. Besides him, Family 5 is responsible for the champions Riverhill Rescuer, Riverhill Ratafia, Swagman from Shiel, Kinnersly Gold Dust, Helensdale Laddie who went to the States and be-

Ch. She's My Fancy at Shelert, a model of conformation and a Group winner.

came one of their leading sires, as did Sigurd of Shelert. Other Shelert champions from this family are the three merle dogs Such a Spree, Streak Lightning, Such a Frolic, and the sables Spark, Special Edition, Sea Urchin, Skirl, Strict Tempo, Sweetsultan, Signature Tune, and Ch.'s Winston of Joywil, Merry Rustler of Myriehewe, Imp of Lynray, Janetstown Journalist and the tricolour Such a Beano at Shelert. Although there are not so many champion bitches there are some very good ones. First to my mind is Ch. She's my Fancy at Shelert, taken all round the best blue merle champion bitch there has been; head properties, colour and make and shape are all first class: she won a Working Group and deserved it. Ch.'s Symphony of Shelert, Samantha of Shelert, Brantcliffe Gem of Love, Shetlo Sheraleigh, (Best in Show winner at the E.S.S.C. Ch. Show), Gay Choice (a Crufts winner.) There are also some good C.C. winning bitches, Sequin of Shelert, Michelmere Luin, Riverhill Robinetta, Such a Myth at Shelert, Shelert's Sweet as Candy and Exbury Perchance to Dream. This family has also produced Moonen Shiel, a Working Trials C.C. winner, and an Ob. Ch. Ghillie of Mospse.

Family 6

Family 6 starts with the Netherkeirs. This was the late Mr Archie Watt's prefix. He was one of the pioneers of the breed.

Netherkeir Cora, a small rich-coloured mahogany sable, was the dam of Riverhill Ruby, a small golden sable and the first home bred Riverhill winner. She was the dam of Ch. Riverhill Rufus and Riverhill Roderick, a C.C. winner. He went to the Shetland Islands. Her daughter Riverhill Rouble was by Ch. Kinnersley Gold Dust, but unlike her sire, who was a lovely red-gold, she was a very heavy-coated, dark-shaded sable with hardly any white. Her show career started quite well and then her ears went flat and that was that. She only had one litter and then went on breeding terms where she was stolen before she could have another litter. So it is through that one litter that Family 6 continues today. It is responsible for two Group winners in Ch. Antoc Sealodge Spotlight and Ch. Deloraine Dilys of Monkswood who is also the dam of Ch. Monkswood Moss Trooper and the dual C.C. winner Lyngold Maestro of Monkswood.

Riverhill Rattle was responsible for Ch. Hallinwood Sealodge Sparkle and Ch. Hallinwood Golden Fetter who bred Ch. Antoc Handclap who went abroad. Fetter was also the great-granddam of Dilys. Another Rattle daughter, Sealodge Single, bred Ch. Antoc Sealodge Spotlight and yet another, Sealodge Sinderella is behing Ch. Greensands Gangster's Moll of Monkswood, a Best in Show at the E.S.S.C. Ch. Show and the dam of Ch. Monkswood Girl Friday of Greensands, a Crufts C.C. winner. Also coming down through Sinderella is Ch. Waindale Minette. Another line coming down from Riverhill Rouble is Ch. Rita of Scalloway who

Ch. Deloraine Dilys of Monkswood, dam of a champion and winner of the Working Group.

has an Ob. C.C. winner descending from her in Rockafella; and a half-sister of Rita, Fancy of Scalloway, a C.C. winner, has two champion dogs stemming from her, Ch. Pruneparks Jason Junior and Ch. Garlea Iona Lad. Another Netherkeir bitch, a half-sister to Cora, was responsible for Ch. Zara of Whytelaw who went to the U.S.A., an Ob. Champion and two C.C. winners but none of them are going on.

Families 7 and 7A

These families produced two important dogs in Ch. Uam Var of Hough-ton Hill and Nutkin of Houghton Hill, nothing else.

Family 8

This is an important family. There are three parts going, 8 and 9 are the two chief Houghton Hill families. In 8 the key bitch is Tango of Houghton Hill, the only black and tan to win a C.C. She had two daughters, Ballet Girl of Houghton Hill and Ch. Mazurka of Houghton Hill. I shall take Ballet Girl first. She was the dam of Ch. Moneyspinner of Exford and her daughter Chorus Girl of Houghton Hill was behind Fetlar Catrina, a C.C. winner, and the dam of Ch. Fetlar Magnus, twice

Ch. Greensands Gangster's Moll of Monkswood, a Best in Show winner at the E.S.S.C. championship show, and already the dam of a champion.

best dog at the E.S.S.C. show before it was raised to championship status. Another daughter, Swasti of Houghton Hill, besides having a daughter Ch. Zephyr of Houghton Hill who is engraved on my memory as she was my best bitch the first time I ever judged, a really beautifully made bitch with quality. Swasti is also behind a lot of famous dogs and bitches including Ch. Tibbetts Lilac, one of the best blue merles, she unfortunately died of distemper after an innoculation break-down; Ch.s Francehill Dry Ginger, now in Canada, Crag of Exford, who went to the States, and Pied Piper of Melvaig; besides several C.C. winners. The latest winners are Ch. Francehill Pin Up and her son Ch. Francehill Persimon.

Another Ballet Girl daughter, Polly Wolly of Houghton Hill, a rather large, showily-marked tricolour, is behind most of the Whytelaws via Merry Maid of Whytelaw, dam of Ch. Laird of Whytelaw, C.C. winner Gay of Whytelaw, Marina of Whytelaw who is behind Ch.s Greenscrees Swordsman, Nobleman and Glamour Girl and Ch. Starbonnie, Gay of Whytelaw is the dam of Ch.s Skye of Whytelaw and Tassel of Whytelaw.

Another of Merry Maid's daughters, Frolic of Whytelaw, is behind the Champions Dryfesdale Gay Girl, Brigdale Renown and Brigdale Romaris from whom is descended two champion dogs in Salroyds Buzzer and Bystars Blakeney and the C.C. winners Ebony Knight of Owlcote and Admyret Ailie. Merry Maid had another daughter Jenny of Whytelaw that produced a C.C. winning daughter in Bridie of Whytelaw, so in all Merry Maid had a champion son and four daughters, one a C.C. winner and the others, all of whom bred champions and C.C. winners, a good record.

A sister of Merry Maid, Lilt of Whytelaw a C.C. winner, had a C.C. winning daughter and is behind two dog champions in Westaglow Nijinski Best in Show at an E.S.S.C. Ch. Show, and Ch. Lythwood Brandysnap.

Another line from Polly Wolly of Houghton Hill comes down through Gaby of Glenholme and via Prospect Fiona, a very nice, bright golden sable who had two C.C.s but failed to get her third. She is behind some very nice bitches, Ch. Brownie of Pitempton, C.C. winners Autumn Glow of Shadynook, Allanvail Gold Star, Crochmaid Serene, Hobby of Flock-

Ch. Dilhorne Blue-mirth, holder of the largest number of bitch C.C.s to date.

fields, Doshell Naiad who is behind Bridgedale Bonny Girl. Hobby of Flockfields dam is also behind Ch. Fairona Rockafella. Another of Gaby's daughters, Netherkeir Maid, is behind two C.C. winning bitches in Shelverne Sonnet and Neartarn Tantrum and also Ch. Snabswood Slainthe.

Tango of Houghton Hill's champion daughter Mazurka of Houghton Hill plays a large part in Family 8. She was a tricolour with a full white collar, very good size and could win today. I always thought her the best of the Houghton Hill champion bitches. She had two daughters; Viola of Houghton Hill who is behind Ch.s Blue Charm of Exford, Dilhorne Bluepuffin, Dilhorne Bluecap, Dilhorne Bluemirth, Helengowan Hera of Hardwick, and the C.C. winners Blue Cloud O'Gruach, Black Ice of Exford, Black Perle of Exford, Tarfin Dazzler, Tarfin Magpie (a black and white), and the dam of Ch. Cregagh Tarfin Blue Melody who is also an Irish champion.

Mazurka's other daughter, Sarabande of Houghton Hill, was the dam of Riverhill Rumba, the first black and white we had ever seen. We bought her at two-day's-old. Mrs Baker said she had never sold a puppy so young before. She was the dam of Riverhill Romantic, a lovely-coloured blue merle who had two C.C.s. The war stopped her getting her third. Her blue merle daughter, Riverhill Rosalind, won the bitch C.C. at the last Kennel Club show ever held. She is behind Ch.'s Hallinwood Flash, Hallinwood Hill Tit Bit and Hallinwood Sweet Trophy and Hallinwood Token. Rather sadly, this part of the family seems to be dormant at the present time.

Family 9

Family 9 contains so many champions that I shall not be able to mention nearly all of them. There are some really lovely ones. It is by far the strongest family at the moment, in the last five years it has produced two thirds of the C.C. winners. It is also the only family to have four generations of champion bitches and no less than five sets of three generations; no other family has any.

It all starts from Ch. Blue Blossom of Houghton Hill who as you can tell by her name, was a blue merle. She was a very attractive bitch, a lovely size and colour. She was the dam of three champions — two dogs and a bitch — Ch. Pea Blossom of Houghton Hill, who had one C.C. winning daughter, Thrift of Houghton Hill, and a daughter, Motley of Houghton Hill, who goes down six generations to Ch. Startler of Exford. But it was from Blue Blossom's non-champion daughters that most of the winners stem. Blue Balloon of Houghton Hill, dam of Ch. Jenny Wren of Crawleyridge CD.Ex UD., who went to the U.S.A. in 1940, and C.C. winner Enchantress of Inchmerry, dam of the first post-war cham-

pion dog, Nuthatch of Larchwood. Another daughter, Sweeze of Houghton Hill, was the dam of Ch. Air Mail of Houghton Hill. Tragedy struck
here; the day after he was made-up and sold to Mrs Miller (Runlee) he
was stolen out of her garden and never seen again.

Sugar Cake of Houghton Hill was another daughter. She bred Ch.
Mime of Houghton Hill and through her daughter, Bon Bon of Hough-
ton Hill, goes down to Ch. Fascinator of Exford and her half-brother
Ch. Exford Piskietye Taw. Fascinator was the dam of Ch. Lothario of
Exford. Her daughter, Joy of Exford, was dam of Ch. Joyful of Exford,
the start of three generations of champions — Blue Bird of Exford, Black
Lace of Exford; and from another daughter, Francehill Glamour of Exford, who started off another one with Ch.s Francehill Glamourous,
Francehill Glamour Girl and Francehill Painted Lady the latter having
a champion grandson in Lirren Evening Shadow at Ramtin. Ch. Francehill Glamorous is also behind Shelridge Liberty Belle, a C.C. winner,
and Ch. Felthorn Beachcomber. Francehill Glamour of Exford had
another daughter, Francehill Hells Bells who goes down to Eltsor Camille,

Ch. Black Lace of
Exford, the last of the
three generation Ex-
ford champion bitches.

Ch. Francehill Glamorous, the first of three generations of Francehill champion bitches.

a blue merle C.C. winner. Joy of Exford, besides being the dam of Joyful, had another daughter, Wren of Umborne, who goes down to Ch. Drumcauchlie Amethyst, also a blue merle. This colour is very strong in this part of the family. Another Fascinator daughter, Fanciful of Exford, is behind Ch. Exford Pipestyle Mystic Star, a lovely tricolour who had a Crufts C.C. and two C.C.s at the E.S.S.C. show to her credit. She is the grand dam of Ch. Nitelife Rogue Star. Going back to Sugar Cake of Houghton Hill, besides Bon Bon she was also the dam of Rill of Houghton Hill who, after eleven generations, came up with Ch. Francehill Fling Low and Ch. Francehill Beach Boy, both very showy golden sables. Returning to Ch. Blue Blossom of Houghton Hill, she had a fifth daughter, Blue Moon of Houghton Hill, who in turn was the dam of Toonie Mona. Now Toonia Mona was a very important lady, a small tricolour, heavy-coated and rather low to the ground with a very good head, a female counterpart of Fydell Startler. She came to Riverhill in the war as an evacuee from the London blitz. She had two litters by Ch. Riverhill Rufus. The first produced Riverhill Rhythmic, the Melvaig foundation bitch. She is behind Ch.s Viking, Honeybunch and Gay Lass, all of

Melvaig, also Ch.s Midnitesun Four Leaf Clover, White Heather, Justin Time, Ch.s Rhinog Waltzing Matilda, Hunky Dory and the Gay Lancer, the Callart Ch.s Miel, Starlight, and Honeyboy, Ch.s Tumblebays Amethyst and Tumblebays Topaz of Monkswood and Monkswood Meridain, Stevlyns Carousel, Stalisfield Moonflower, Ch.s Kyleburn Golden Eagle, Penny Royal, Wild Thyme and Athena, also several C.C. winners.

The other two sisters were Riverhill Roundel, who is behind Ch. Budlet of Surreyhills and Riverhill Rhapsody, dam of Riverhill Rival, the sire of Ch. Butterfly of Exford and his sister Riverhill Ritourndle who must have been the first post-war export as she went to Belgium in 1945. Toonie Mona was also the dam of Toonie Herepanda who is behind Ch. Bramble of Wytchfields and Ch. Francis of Merrion.

Riverhill Rouge, from Toonie Mona's first litter, was a 13-inch sable with a lovely little one-piece head and natural ears. She had her sires sweet expression and good eye. As a four-day-old puppy she had a narrow escape. A dog got into the room her mother was nursing four puppies in and there was a bit of a kerfuffle. When we had got the dog out and went to see that the puppies were all right there were only three. The dog puppy, who was his mother's favourite, had vanished. We could only think she had swallowed him to save him when the stranger came in. It's a thing that has never happened to us before, or since thank goodness. I hate to think what would have happened if it had been Rouge that had gone. The breed would never have had some of its most famous dogs. Rouge has so many winners descended from her that she heads Part II of Family 9.

Rouge was the dam of Ch. Riverhill Redcoat. She had three daughters that go on. Riverhill Rebecula who has no less than three obedience champions descended from her and one show champion. Another daughter Bothkennar's Riverhill Round Off, also had an obedience champion and goes down to Ch. Danvis Rhapsody and Ch.s Greenscrees Lynda Girl, Dunbrae Golden Bianco, Sumburgh Little Hercules, Sumburgh Tesoro Zhivago. The third Rouge daughter was Riverhill Red Biddy. She in turn had three daughters; Riverhill Red Gold, Rara Avis and Red Riding Hood. The latter has three champions and two C.C. winners descending from her but all of them dogs. Rara Avis is behind Oastwood Tia Maria, a duel C.C. winner, one of them at Crufts; but it was Riverhill Red Gold who was by Ch. Riverhill Rikki (who we have always considered technically our best champion) mated to Ch. Alasdair of Tintobank who produced the record making Ch. Riverhill Rare Gold.

Lucy, as she was known to all her friends, was the most remarkable bitch. Having nearly died of hepatitis when a few months old (there was no inoculation for it at that time) she went — at nine months — Best Bitch in Show at the Ladies Kennel Association. This was before the days of groups. The judge told me afterwards that if she had not thrown it up at the last moment she would have been Best in Show, but as she was only such a baby at the time it wasn't surprising she'd tired. At her next show she was again best bitch, all breeds, and her third C.C. was won at the E.S.S.C. championship show.

But it was as a brood bitch she made her greatest impact on the breed. She had four champion daughters, all by different dogs, and four other daughters who bred on; and one C.C. winning son, Riverhill Rolling Home. Her eldest daughter Ch. Riverhill Real Gold had a C.C. winning daughter, Riverhill Ring of Gold, who in turn was the grandmother of Ch. Riverhill Ring the Bell, Best of Breed at Crufts Centenary Show There are several C.C. winners half-brothers and sisters from this line. Real Gold had a litter sister Riverhill Reis who had a C.C. winning descendant in Vaila Easter Advocaat. The second litter produced Ch. Riverhill Ready Cash who had two C.C. winning children, her litter sisters Riverhill Rare Bird had a champion son Kinreen Blue Kestrel and a daughter Riverhill Rare Lark who is behind a lot of champions and C.C. winners, Ch.s Rodhill Clouded Yellow and Clouded Dawn, Lyngold

Ch. Riverhill Ring the Bell C.C. Best of Breed at Crufts Centenary Show, 1973. She is the great-great-grand-daughter of Ch. Riverhill Rare Gold.

Blue Zinnia, Monkswood Made of Money CD.Ex, Drannoc Susiley Space Girl, Stormane Shining Light. The third litter was Ch. Riverhill Rather Rich. She herself produced four champions and so had two lots of three generations of champion bitches, and her daughter, Ch. Riverhill Rather Nice, produced the first and only fourth generation champion bitch in Ch. Riverhill Rather Special. Besides Rather Nice she had Ch. Riverhill Rather Dark who had a duel C.C. winning son in Riverhill Riccory and a C.C. winning great-great-grand-daughter. Rather Rich had two champion sons in Riverhill Raider and Riverhill Richman, and another daughter Riverhill Rich Fare who had Ch. Riverhill Rapparee who went to Sweden. Rather Nice also had a champion son in Riverhill Rampion who went to Australia where he proved the top sire for several years running. The fourth litter produced Ch. Riverhill Rarity of Glenmist,

First of three generations of champion bitches; Ch. Riverhill Rare Gold, Ch. Riverhill Rarity of Glenmist, Ch. Gypsy Star of Glenmist.

who in turn had Ch. Gypsy Star of Glenmist and was the first third generation of champion bitches. Also coming from this line is Ch. Shelfrect Sunlit Suzanne and Ch. Glenmist Gaylord of Jaylea and a C.C. winner in Glenmist Lorna Doone of Jefsfire. This litter also had Riverhill Rare Romance who in turn had C. Riverhill Runaway Match dam of Ch. Riverhill Rash Promise, who bred Riverhill Rash Chatter the dam of Ch. Riverhill Ricotta. Rash Promise's other C.C. winning daughter was Riverhill Rapid. Riverhill Rolling Home was also one of this litter. The fifth litter produced Shiel's Riverhill Real Kindness who is behind Ch.s Parrocks Nohow, Parrocks Possibility, Parrock Red Dragoon and Scylla Snow Violet. Riverhill Ranger was in this litter. In all, Rare Gold, through her daughters, has thirty-eight champions and nineteen C.C. winners descended from her; and through her two sons, Riverhill Rolling Home and Riverhill Ranger, over eighty champions and C.C. winners. Rare Gold herself had twenty-nine puppies and reared twenty-seven of them. Of these, twenty won prizes at championship shows and open shows. At one championship show the dog C.C. winner was by one son, the Res C.C. by another, and the bitch C.C. was out of one daughter and the Res C.C. out of another. I should think this is a record for any breed. She has winning descendants in every

The four top dogs at the Three Counties Show in 1963, the year they all became champions. Swagman from Shiel R.C.C., Antoc Sealodge Spotlight C.C., Riverhill Runaway Match C.C. and Riverhill Rather Nice R.C.C. They are all grandchildren of Riverhill Rare Gold.

country where there are Shelties. When judging in Denmark not so long ago my Best of Breed was Danish bred but on looking up his pedigree later I found Rare Gold was on both sides of it. Rare Gold really was gold in colour but it was her expression that got you. People used to stop us in the street to say what a lovely face she had. As to character, you could only describe her by saying she was a darling. Certainly as long as there are Shelties she will be remembered. Rare Gold had a litter sister Riverhill Realgar. She is behind two C.C. winners and one of the latest champions in Forestland Briar.

Family 10

Family 10 started with a Rough Collie called Floss. It produced Ch. Specks of Mountfort, Ch. Gawaine of Camelaird, Ch. Lochinvar of Clerwood and three C.C. Clerwood bitches. Unfortunately none of them bred on.

Family 11

Family 11 had some early champion dogs. The most important was Ch. Eltham Park Eureka, two Dryfesdale champions in Dream Girl and Daisy, two C.C. bitches in Dryfesdale Dawn and Diamond and Ch. Garniehill Tulyar and Ch. Helengowan Striking. None of the dogs have gone on.

Family 12

Family 12 had two early champions in Ch. Kilravoch Goldfinder and Ch. Margawse of Camelaird and some C.C. winners. Since the war it is responsible for Fydell Startler and a lovely champion bitch in Michelmere Sona and her daughter Michelmere Daffin. Unfortunately their line has died out.

Family 13

This is an active family and has two parts going. The key bitch is Winnie of Abelour who had three daughters: Wendy of Abelour was the dam of Ch. Fydell Round Up, Linda of Abelour who is behind Ch. Foxlark Fandango, Laura of Kinslady, and Helensdale Aviatrix who is the most important. She had six daughters, two of them C.C. winners. One of them, Helensdale Hazel, goes down to Ch. Kyleburn Star Sound. Helensdale Gentle Lady was the dam of Ch. Helensdale Bhan and Ch. Helensdale Ace and through her daughters Helensdale Shona is behind Ch. Penvose Brandy Snap and a dual C.C. winner Mywicks Wattagem who

Ch. Riverhill Rare
Gold – the most
successful bitch of all
time.

Ch. Sumburgh Sirius
and his dam, Ch.
Helensdale Vanessa.

went abroad. Then there was Fydell Satisfaction who is behind six champions, four of them bitches, and four C.C. winners. The only one to have bred on is Ch. Shady Fern of Sheldawyn, a golden sable of great quality. Another Aviatrix daughter was Helensdale Hostess who had two beautiful champion grand-daughters, Helensdale Wendy and Wax-wing. I gave them both C.C.s. Unfortunately for this country, they both went overseas. The line goes on through a great-grand-daughter Ch. Helensdale Vanessa, the last of the Helensdale champions but owned and shown by Mrs Morewood. She had a champion son Sumburgh Sirius and a grand-daughter Sumburgh Maggie May who was a C.C. winner. Vanessa has four champion dogs descended from her Ch.s Scarabrae Sinjon and Statesman, Bridgdale Play Boy and Shelderon Gay Ghillie and a C.C. bitch winner Sumburgh Witch Hazel. The sixth Aviatrix daughter, Iris of Knockmahar was a wolf sable. Again, most of her champion descendants are dogs — an impressive lot too — Ch.s Watta-woodcut, Ireland's Eve Trefoil of Arolla, Hightown Majestic Lad, Hazelhead Gay Wanderer, Durnovaria Double O Seven, Durnovaria Double Agent, Shauntree's Jamie of Sunbower, Marksman of Ellendale. Her three champion bitch descendants are Ch.s Joyful of Durnovaria, Ellendale Prim of Plovern and Pippet of Plovern, grand-dam of Ellendale

Traveller a C.C. winner who is now in Australia. Iris had one champion daughter, Cutie of Knockmahar, a very attractive bitch but one who took a scunner to me and, on the two occasions I judged her, refused to let me touch her. She had a wolf sable C.C. winning son, Rhinog Pimpernel. Winnie of Abelour's daughter Laura of Kinslady produced a champion daughter in Ch. Fair Sheena and a daughter Lydwell Beauty who is behind two champion dogs, Arolla Ebony of Wallerscote and Tyneford Tarsus and a C.C. winner and three C.C. winning bitches, none who have bred on.

Families 14 and 15

Families 14 and 15 only went on for four generations.

Family 16

Family 16 comes through Ch. Freshfield Fad, the dog picked off the streets of Aberdeen and made a champion by a Collie breeder for a bet. Anyhow, however it started it has been very successful and is going on today through Ch. Willowstone Wanderer and Ch. Black Swan of Scylla. It also contains most of the Callart champions coming through Heatherbell of Callart — Russetcoat, Orpheus, Struan, Diadem and Star Princess, as well as Ch.s Luna Andy and Duffus of Upperslaughter and Ch. Blairside Dream Girl, a very attractive little golden sable who got her name in the papers as she was stolen off her bench at a show but was luckily recovered. Ch. Scylla Vaguely Blue and Ch. Cowellekot Crown Prince of Stormane are the latest champions in this line.

Families 17, 18, 19, 20, 21, 22, 23 and 25 have all died out.

Family 24

Family 24 is very active. It got going with two litter sisters, both blue merles out of a tricolour bitch called Voe who came from Shetland. She was mated to Tilford Blue Beau, a son of the merle Collie Mountlethen Blue Prince which is where the colour came from. One was Mary of the Wansdyke, the dam of the first Sheltie I ever owned. His sister was bought by Mr R. Taylor and called Fionie of Wyndora. She was tricolour and bred a C.C. winning tricolour daughter Wishing of Wyndora, who bred a really lovely bitch, Ch. Wevonne of Wyndora. Unfortunately she got made up in 1939 and was sold to some people who lived on the Isle of Wight and they never bred from her, a great pity but times were difficult once the war started. Wishing also had another C.C. winner,

Heatherbell of Callart,
a very successful
brood bitch.

Wrina of Wyndora. Fionie had another daughter, Wishes of Wyndora, who bred on to two C.C. winning bitches and two C.C. dog winners, but it isn't active at the moment. Mary's sister, Riverhill Rosette, the first Riverhill bitch, had two litters to Ch. Gawaine of Camelaird, much against his owner Mrs Allen's will. She thought it dreadful to mate a merle to a sable but we were so charmed by Gawaine we were determined to use him and we never regretted it. One litter produced Riverhill Rosamund, a sable merle who is behind Hildlane Cloudy Sky the dam of Ch. Hildlane Minstrel Knight and Ch. Francehill Hildlane Blue Cavalier, and also the C.C. winning bitch Hildlane Misty Dawn, the dam of Ch.

Riverhill Roguish who is behind most of Family 24.

Hildlane Winters Night. Also from this line came Dippersmore Debutant of Jefsfire who won the C.C. at Crufts. Unfortunately she had been sold to go abroad before the show. Rosette's other daughter by Gawaine was Riverhill Russett, who actually had been promised to a cousin when a small pup but Patience fell for her and we had to produce another pup to take her place. Lucky we did as she is behind the greatest part of Family 24. Her great-grand-daughter Riverhill Roguish was a remarkable bitch; a blue merle though neither parent was a blue merle. She was born during one of the worst daylight raids in 1940, whelped a litter when flying bombs were exploding all round, but she was never in the slightest bit gun shy. She turned into a wonderful worker, could hold up a yard of bullocks, kill a rat as well as any terrier, and was a wonderful mother – in fact she had only to hear a puppy cry and whose ever it was she would bring up whatever she had last eaten for it. She had six daughters that bred on and one champion son, Riverhill Reefer of Exford, who went to Germany.

Her daughters were Riverhill Risible who is behind the two Dilhorne champions, Blue Midnight and Blue Nobleman, Riverhill Railery behind

Granthrope Garla a dual C.C. winner; Riverhill Razzle had a C.C. winning son and daughter, Caitiff and Candy of Inchmerry. Riverhill Romp had a C.C. winning son, Sea Boots from Shiel and a great-grand-daughter Vennards Benedictine who won the bitch C.C. at the first championship E.S.S.C. show and then died of distemper. Shiels Riverhill Riotous grand-dam of Riverhill Remarkable, who is behind Ch. Janlynns Candy Kisses and is dam of Ch. Riverhill Respectable. But the daughter whose line is going strongest was Riverhill Reticent, the grand-dam of Ch. Riverhill Rugosa. Except that she was a shaded sable and not a merle, Rugosa resembled her ancestor, Roguish, in many ways. She could run down a rabbit in the open and kill it, a thing I've never seen another Sheltie do. She had two litters, both by Ch. Riverhill Redcoat. The first litter produced Ch. Riverhill Rikki and the bitches Riverhill Roselet and Shiel's Riverhill Rosita. Roselet is behind Ch. Riverhill Rogue and the dual C.C. winner Riverhill Rose Diamond who has a C.C. winning dog Riverhill Roquefort and the bitch, Ballerina of Rhinog. Rosita has three C.C. winners stemming from her; Corncrest Katrina, Elanmore Cotton Queen and Elenmore Carnival Time. From the second litter came River-hill Rosalie one of the Shelert foundation bitches. From her stem some of the famous champion bitches, Slipper Satin, Shahreen, So Time Flies, Silken Sari, Such a Gay Time, Sands of Delight, Bezzibruk Cour-telle and the champion dogs Spice, Shantung, Sail Ho and Sinbad the Sailor, and also eleven C.C. winners.

The second daughter from the second litter was Riverhill Roseate who had two daughters, Rosetta and Rosabel. The first is behind Ch. Riverhill Riddle and Ch. Ellington Endless Folly who ended up in Norway. Rosabel is responsible for Ch. Christie of Tooneytown and so is behind the Loughrigg champions Day Festivity of Lysebourne, Dragon Fly, Kings Minstrel and Cregagh Student Prince who is also an Irish champion; also the C.C. winners Loughrigg First Sea Saga, and Cregagh Loughrigg Harbour Nymph. Day Festivity is behind Ch. Lysebourne Sea Nymph and the two champion dogs Mistmere Marching Orders and Mistmere Marking Time at Stornaway. There should be no danger of this family dying out.

11 The Working Sheltie

The first obedience tests in this country started in the early 1920s. They were more or less confined to Alsatians. When other breeds were able to take part Shelties got their foot in. Mrs Raike's little sable and white bitch Bundle and Go did very well and won several tests. She was always a great favourite with the onlookers as she was small and a cheerful worker.

After her, came Miss Bignold's blue merle Christopher Robin. We took a great interest in this dog as we bred him from our first bitch, Riverhill Rosette. He was by Peabody Paul. Rather an interesting thing colour-wise here was that Rosette's litter sister Mary of the Wansdyke was also mated to Peabody Paul. She had four blue merles and one tricolour. Our Rosette had four tricolours and one blue merle, Christopher Robin. It just shows what tricky things merles are to breed.

Christopher Robin won quite well in obedience and also in the show ring. He was also a very good working dog on the farm.

In 1936 Miss Osborne's Moonen Shiel appeared on the scene. She was the first Sheltie to qualify CD.Ex (Companion Dog gaining 80 per cent marks) and UD.Ex (Utility Dog gaining 80 per cent marks). In 1939 she won the Working Trials C.C., the first time a small dog had done so. In doing this she had to get over a 6 foot (180 cm) fence and do a 9-foot-long (approx. 270 cm) jump retrieving an eight ounce weight over the high jump. This was the standard for Alsatians and no allowances were made for the Sheltie's size. In her two-hour cold mile-long track she gained 383 out of 385 points. She also won the open class at the 1939 Cruft's and ended up CD.Ex, UD.Ex and TD.Ex (Trial Dog gaining 80 per cent marks).

Her training in track work stood Miss Osborne in good stead as one day after walking with the dogs for hours on Kenley Common in bracken and heather she returned to her car to find she had lost the car keys. Shiel was sent to seek and after twenty minutes came back with the keys in her mouth, much to the relief of her owner who was wondering if she would have to spend the night out!

Miss Osborne also had a large tricolour bitch, Maramore CD.Ex, and she trained Col. the Hon. B. Russell's Ch. Jenny Wren of Crawleyridge. Jenny Wren qualified CD.Ex and UD. She later became the only international C.D. in the breed as at the beginning of the war she was sent over to the States and continued to work over there. She failed to get her show championship as she had two very bright blue eyes and they were not acceptable to the Americans at that time.

Other Shelties to do well were Fetlar Merilees, Sea Mist from Shiel, Toonie Bridget of Crawleyridge who got a U.S.A. CD.Ex. She went out with Jenny Wren. Golden Boy of Inchmery, who had two C.C.s, also had his working career cut short by the war. Mrs Uglione's Folette Romana CD.Ex was a live wire sable, not much bigger than a large Papillon. She darted about the ring and brought the house down.

But all obedience work came to a stop when war started. The first Sheltie to do well after the war was Mrs Montgomery's Melcettes Sea Spray CD.Ex, a blue merle. An interesting thing about this bitch was that her dam was Northern Mist, another blue merle. Northern Mist was Ch. Dilhorne Norseman of Melvaig's great-great-great-grand-dam and he of course was a genuine working sheepdog as well as being a show champion.

Mrs Glasse, besides having the first bitch obedience champion in

Ch. Monkswood Made of Money, a CD. Ex.

Honour Bright of Surreyhills, also had the first show champion to get a CD.Ex, Ch. Budlet of Surreyhills. He was by Ch. Riverhill Rescuer. I have a private theory about Rescuer. He is behind a great many of the obedience dogs who have done well and though he was sable and we knew his forebears for several generations, and they were all sable or tricolour, he sired a great many black and whites, in fact to one sable bitch all the puppies were black and white. Now this was the original colour of the old dogs and I feel, because he carried this factor, he may have carried the working ability too.

It wasn't till the fifties that the first dog obedience champion appeared in Master Ian, owned by Mr Ratcliffe who also made up his son, Ob. Ch. Ghillie of Mospe who in turn sired Ob. Ch. Masterpiece of Mospe who was out of Ob. Ch. Yelruth Annfield who was out of Riverhill Rail, a granddaughter of Riverhill Rouge and the latest obedience champion, Our Shep, also goes back to Rouge, as does Ob. Ch. Black Diamond of Bothkennar. So Family 9 is responsible for some of the best obedience dogs as well as the top show dogs.

Another obedience champion daughter of Rescuer was Ob. Ch. Safety First from Shiel. She was twice third at Cruft's, in 1958 and 1959. Whilst doing distant control, she used to amuse the spectators by 'swearing' under her breath at her owner, Mrs McMillan.

At the moment there are a lot of dogs who have qualified to enter Test C at championship obedience shows where OCs can be won. The latest show champion to qualify CD.Ex, UD.Ex is Ch. Monkswood Made of Money. Her daughter, Moccas Cashierd, is also CD.Ex and has two C.C.s in Breed Classes. She too comes from Family 9.

In 1975 a sable dog called Rockafella won two Ob. C.C.s and so was able to take part at Crufts, where he lost only 2½ marks out of three hundred and finished tying for fifth place amongst the best dogs in the country. Again in 1978 another Sheltie, Golden Gregory, took part at Crufts and finished joint sixth. There have been two bitches who have won C.C.s, Rainelor Raven in 1978 and the latest, Rodhill Frosted Cherry. She has a kennel mate Rockaround Marble Cloud who qualified for championship class at seventeen months and at her first championship show, when only eighteen months, was placed fourth. This is believed to be the youngest Sheltie ever to qualify and be placed in a championship class, so Shelties are keeping their end up against the very hottest competition.

So much for the Sheltie in obedience work. But what about general farm work? There is no doubt that the instinct to work sheep or cattle is still very strong in some Shelties. The classic example was Ch. Dilhorne Norseman of Melvaig. As I have mentioned before, he worked a flock of several hundred sheep on his owner's farm and also managed to be best

Rohill Frosted Cherry
Obd. C.C. and Rock-
around Marble Cloud.

of breed at Cruft's and the E.S.S.C. championship show. But on the
whole the show Sheltie is a little on the small side to work large sheep
— Shetland sheep are very small.

We ourselves have had an outstanding worker, Riverhill Roguish. Her sire was black and white and her dam went back to Island stock. During the war when working on the farm we could safely leave her in charge of a yard full of bullocks while we brought in fodder. If we had had sheep, I am quite sure she would have worked them. She was also a really first class ratter, as good as any Terrier. She is behind many of the present-day winners including Ob. Ch. Safety First from Shiel.

We sold one puppy and were later told by her delighted owner that she was the 'best sheepdog in Northampton'. Several others have gone to cowmen and we have had good reports about them. So Shelties still retain their ability to be useful on a farm.

12   A Glossary of Terms

PART 1

KENNEL CLUB C.C.: Challenge Certificate. This is allocated by the Kennel Club at championship shows, one for each sex. A dog must win at least three under different judges, and one must be won as an adult, i.e. when over a year old, to qualify for the title of champion. There is no limit to the number of C.C.s a dog can win as a puppy but the title of champion is not awarded till he has won one as an adult.

B.i.S.: Best in Show.

B.o.B.: Best of Breed.

B.o.S.: Best of Opposite Sex.

N.A.F.: Put after a dog's name on a show entry form and catalogue if a name has been applied for but not yet been passed by the Kennel Club at date of entry. There have been some mix-ups with this; one Sheltie won a C.C. under a N.A.F. name and later appeared under a different name and again won a C.C. This caused a rumpus among other exhibitors till they were told the Kennel Club had refused to pass the first name.

T.A.F.: Put on the entry form and in the catalogue when a registered dog has been bought and the transfer of ownership has not yet been approved by the Kennel Club.

JUNIOR WARRANT: An award offered by the Kennel Club for dogs under eighteen months. The dog must win not less than 25 points at open and championship shows in breed classes. A first prize counts as one point at an open show and three points at a championship show. The Junior Warrant must be claimed from the Kennel Club, giving shows and classes where the points were won.

AFFIX, SUFFIX: A regulation has been brought out by the Kennel Club re registrations:

'The Committee may grant an application to register an affix so as to give the grantee, during the continuance of the grant, sole right to use such affix as part of the name when registering or changing the name of a dog. The grantee may not dispose or attempt to dispose of an affix

without the consent of the Committee. Where the grantee of a registered affix wishes to utilise it when registering or changing the name of a dog solely and unconditionally his property it must be used as a prefix, that is to say as the first word in the name of the dog (a) was bred by him or (b) was bred from parents each of which was bred by him. Otherwise it must be used as a suffix, that is to say the last word in the name.'
(reproduced by Courtesy of the Kennel Club.)

That is to say, a dog bred by owner or when both parents were bred by him would be registered as Riverhill Romantic, if not bred by owner as Romantic of Riverhill.

This regulation has been brought in to stop people buying in stock unrelated to their own dogs, putting their kennel name on it and selling abroad to unsuspecting people who imagine, as it carries their kennel name, that it will be their breeding.

Note: Kennels who had had suffixes for some years were able to carry on using them until 31st, December, 1976 if they applied to do so before 31st December, 1971.

BREEDER'S DIPLOMA: This is a thing you can apply to the Kennel Club for if you have bred a puppy, sold it and the new owner shows it and makes it a champion.

STUD BOOK ENTRIES: If you have a dog that wins a C.C. or reserve C.C. or is 1st, 2nd or 3rd in the open classes at a championship show, it gets a new number which goes into the Kennel Club *Stud Book*. When this happens the dog's name cannot be altered after thirty days have elapsed from the date of the first win which qualifies it or any of its progeny for entry in the Kennel Club *Stud Book*. The limit class wins have been stopped by the Kennel Club.

PART 2

Head

APPLE HEAD: The back skull is rounded and there is usually a high stop.

ONE-PIECE: Looked at from the front should run up in one smooth line to the ears.

BUILT-UP: When the foreface is very full right up under the eyes, very often making the eyes look as if they were in tunnels.

STOP: The rise between the lower part of the head (foreface) and the back skull. It should be between the eyes.

ROMAN NOSE: When the foreface has a convex curve from stop to nostril; very ugly.

DROOPY NOSE: When the cartilage of the nostrils droops down, not to be confused with a roman nose where the whole foreface is curved.

RECEDING SKULL: When the head slopes backwards from the stop to the ears.

PLAIN FACE: Not an ugly dog but one with no white markings on its head.

DISHED FACE: When the face is slightly concaved, giving the impression that the nose is a little tip-tilted. It gives the dog a merry expression but is not a good show point.

CLEAN HEAD: Not a newly washed head but one that is smooth all over, i.e. no veins or lumps and bumps or prominent eyebrows or cheeks.

CHEEKY: When the cheek bones bulge outwards and spoil the flat sides of the head.

BALANCED HEAD: One in which the skull and foreface are each of the same length, the head looking in perfect proportion.

COW EARS: Rather large and set on the side of the head. Very often the tip, instead of falling over forward, is twisted sideways.

LOW OR FLAT EARS: When they fall down flat against the head or more than the tips fall over.

STRAIGHT THROUGH: As applied to a head when the dog has no stop, the line from the nose to the top of the head is dead flat.

PIG JAW: The teeth are level but the lower jaw is very shallow and slopes away under the chin.

BAD MOUTH: Overshot or undershot, that is the top jaw is longer than the bottom and vice-versa.

Body

STRAIGHT SHOULDERS: When the shoulder blade is not set at an angle of 45 degrees. You can have the shoulder blade set at the right angle and yet have a straight upper arm. This is from the lower point of the shoulder blade to the elbow. This is the most prevalent fault in the breed today and accounts for the impeded movement one sees such a lot of.

STRAIGHT FRONT: Not to be confused with a straight shoulder; the front is the two front legs. The shafts of the legs should be straight when looked at from the front; but sideways-on the legs should not run straight down into the feet — there should be a slope at the pastern where it meets the feet.

SLAB SIDED: When the rib cage is flat and there is no outward curve to the rib bones.

HERRING GUTTED: When the body runs up under the loins and the dog appears to have no belly.

SHORT OF A RIB: When there appears to be a gap between the last rib and hips.

GOOSE RUMPED: When the loins are higher than the withers; very ugly.

SWAY BACKED: When there is a pronounced dip between the withers and the loins.

WELL BODIED UP: The opposite of immature.

LIGHT IN CONDITION: Too thin.

RACY: A dog with graceful lines that looks like being able to gallop.

WORKMANLIKE: A sound, well-made and balanced dog standing four square with good bone.

CAT FEET: Very short round feet, no length in the toes.

HARE FEET: The opposite to cat feet, the toes long and rather flat and pointed.

FURNISHINGS: The frills of a Sheltie in full coat, on chest, forelegs, hindquarters and tail.

ON THE BLOW: When the coat is about to moult out.

GAY TAIL: One carried too high above the level of the back.

KINKED TAIL: When one or more vertibrae are displaced in the tail, leaving a lump on the bone. This is very hereditary and not to be confused with a curly tail when the end turns up or over.

COW HOCKED: When the hocks are nearly touching and the hind feet turn outwards.

STRAIGHT STIFLE: Where there is no curve in the stifle and it runs more or less straight to the hock.

CHIPPENDALE FRONT: When the shafts of the front legs bow outwards and then in below the knee.

TOES IN: This can be done both in front and behind. Sometimes described as pigeon-toes in front, it usually goes with being out at elbows. Behind the toes go in and the hocks are apart. Usually dogs that do this are very fast and good jumpers but it is not very pretty.

SOUND: When a dog is described as being sound it does not just mean that the dog is not lame. A sound dog is well-made, stands four-square, has no bad faults, i.e. bad mouth, kinked tail, etc.

LACKS QUALITY: Means coarse in skull, large round eyes and heavy coarse bone; ungraceful.

NICELY BROKEN UP: Used to describe blue merles, meaning the black patches are not too big and are well placed.

WELL LET DOWN: Applied to hocks, when the stifle is well bent and comes down in a sweep to the hocks so that they are not a long way from the ground as in the case of a straight stifle.

MADE UP: This does not refer to cosmetics but means the dog has won his third C.C. and so becomes a champion.

BY: This is the sire, i.e. by Ch. Helensdale Ace.

OUT OF OR EX: This is the dam, i.e. out of Helensdale Gentle Lady, You would think this is pretty self-evident but it is surprising how many breeders who ought to know better get this wrong and talk about a puppy being by its dam or out of its sire.

Index